SHADOWS, DARKNESS, *and* DAWN

A Lenten Journey with Jesus

THOMAS R. STEAGALD

D1302274

UPPER
ROOM BOOKS®
NASHVILLE

Cover image: iStock
Cover design: Marc Whitaker, MTW Design / www.mtwdesign.net
Interior design: PerfecType, Nashville, TN
First printing: 2010

Library of Congress Cataloging-in-Publication Data
Steagald, Thomas R.
  Shadows, darkness, and dawn : a Lenten journey with Jesus / Thomas R. Steagald.
    p. cm.
  ISBN 978-0-8358-1032-6
  1. Lent—Meditations. 2. Bible. N.T. Gospels—Meditations. 3. Jesus Christ—Biography—Meditations. 4. Common lectionary (1992) I. Title.
  BV85.S675 2010
  242'.34—dc22   2010020339

Printed in the United States of America

To the Saints of Lafayette Street United Methodist Church
sudden and unexpected dawn after a long, dark night.

So deeply do we care for you that we are determined
to share with you not only the gospel of God but also our own selves,
because you have become very dear to us.

1 Thessalonians 2:8

Contents

O give thanks to the L<small>ORD</small> . . .

who led his people through the wilderness,

for his steadfast love endures forever.

—Psalm 136:1a, 16

Acknowledgments

I have long noticed an unavoidable, if unintended, conceit suggested by the acknowledgments page of a book. Indeed, only the author might imagine that anything of consequence has been accomplished that would demand or even justify such public thanks.

Still, most authors *feel*, and especially after long months and even years of labor, that *something* has been birthed anyway. No surprise then that we can't suppress the urge to hand out, as it were, cigars to those who have told us to push, to rest, to breathe, to scream if we have to, to get the baby out and into the light of day. And so I grant myself an indulgence for such giddy whimsy.

Thanks, then, to Anne Trudel, Robin Pippin, and Jeannie Crawford-Lee of Upper Room Books—it was my honor and pleasure to work with you three. Thanks once again to Rachelle Gardner and Liz Heaney who, while they had nothing specific to do with this book, helped me find voice and vocation as a writer. I love you both.

Thanks to the congregation of First United Methodist Church of Stanley, North Carolina, for patiently listening as I first worked through some of this material in preaching and teaching. Thanks also to the Lafayette Street United Methodist Church—to whom the book is dedicated—for patience and understanding as I scrambled to finish among them what I had started with others.

Deep gratitude to those who read all or parts of the manuscript and helped me avoid serious embarrassment: Dr. Jeff Patterson, Veranita Alvord,

Joe Tarpley, Dr. Laura Smith, Saxon Scarborough, Terry Bevill, Steve Lee, Doris Taylor and, not least, my wife, Jo. Whatever little embarrassments remain accrue to me alone.

Thanks to Tabitha Owens, my assistant in Stanley, and Fran Davis, my assistant in Shelby, who guarded me as I worked. Thanks to David and Lissa Brashear, and to Paul and Ruth McLarty, who gave me wonderful places when I needed to get away to think and write.

Thanks to Jo, again, and to my wonderful children, Bethany and Jacob, who keep me honest when I have a deadline to meet—and are often willing to eat supper when I can take a break. And RIP, Chester, who curled up between my legs as long as he could and ever invited me to soothe my frustrations by rubbing his back and ears. I miss you, puppy dog.

Invitation

To dwell in this desert and make it bloom requires that we indulge in neither guilt nor vainglorious fantasizing, but struggle to know ourselves as we are. In this process we will not escape sadness and pain.

—Kathleen Norris

Lent begins on Ash Wednesday and lasts through Maundy Thursday. The forty days of Lent (Sundays are exempt from the tabulation) call to mind Noah's rainy season, the Hebrews' years of sojourn beyond the Red Sea, the generations of Israel's exile in Babylon—and, of course, Jesus' trek into the wilderness before he began his public ministry.

To do all that God wanted him to do, to be for God all he wanted to be, Jesus had to face the Tempter and his temptations. Jesus had to name—both for himself and against his Adversary—who he was, whom he served. His days in the wilderness were purgative, then, as all lesser, self-serving options were considered and cast aside, but also formative: not this, but this.

He fasted, and in the midst of physical weakness found spiritual strength. He remembered the stories of Israel, and in God's ongoing purposes found his own place and purpose.

Before any of the many he had come to serve had time enough or opportunity to tell him who he needed to be—who they *wanted* him to be—Jesus already knew who he was and who he wasn't.

Jesus' time in the wilderness provided clarity for his life and work.

Almost ever since, in hopes for similar clarity, followers of Jesus have embraced his example of separation, privation, and prayer. Some have gone on pilgrimage to the Holy Land, on mission trips, or to monasteries. Many more have determined to observe a holy Lent in other ways—to set aside as best they can the noises and busyness of the world and refocus. Lenten pilgrims take themselves away from the "crowds" in one fashion or another and set aside the clutter of their lives, to spend more time alone with God.

Which is not to say Lent is an entirely solitary discipline. Alone as he was in the wilderness, Jesus was also attended by angels (Mark 1:13). We are not alone either. We typically make our Lenten "vows" in the congregation on Ash Wednesday, and we continue our weekly rhythms of worship and Bible study, choir, and service. That said, Lent may be an intensely personal exercise. When we intensify our devotion; our self-examination and repentance; our prayer, fasting, and self-denial; our reading and meditation on God's Word[1]—these gestures, taken together, express a serious commitment and sacrifice.

––––

The Temple in Jerusalem was the center of Jewish life and worship from the time of Solomon until its destruction by the Romans in 70 CE. Pilgrimage to the Temple, by both Jews and Gentiles, was constant, but not everyone was allowed close proximity. For the sake of maintaining its ritual purity the Temple was heavily fortified, guarded not only by troops but also by tradition and regulation. And yet, for all the restrictions, there was from the start one type of sacrifice even Gentiles were allowed to offer at the Temple: a "burnt offering," an *olah*.

The *olah* was offered for three reasons: as a sign of intimacy between the worshiper and God; as a demonstration of the worshiper's devotion; and as a prayer for the forgiveness of sins. Over time, for most worshipers, the last became first, so to speak. That is, the desire for expiation, the prayer for forgiveness, came to be regarded as the primary purpose for the *olah*. But in fact many Jewish teachers, past and present, have regarded intimacy with God as the primary benefit and result of sacrifice.

If in some places and times Lenten tradition too has been mostly draped in sackcloth, intimacy with God is our real desire. Even that desire, however, is derivative. In the same way, we love God because God first loved us (1 John 4:19). We desire intimacy with God because God first and eternally desires intimacy with us—which is to say, with all the children of creation.

Each day, in the cool of the evening, God entered the Garden to savor the intimacies that can be afforded only by separation. Sadly, tragically, the good separations became a horrible breach. Intimacy was ruptured, and the relationship between God and our parents was sundered. We have all been looking for Eden ever since—which is not a place, of course, but the relationship, the intimacy, the communion for which we were created and for which we still long.

We live in the shadows of that lost Day.

During Lent we acknowledge those shadows, both in our world and in ourselves. We try to see and name them for what they are, not as an act of self-loathing but as a prayer to find, kindle, and explore deeper intimacy with God. We believe that we come to the darkened Garden at all because God calls to us, that we desire reunion with God because God has gone ahead of us—has taken up residence in the shadows of our world and heart in Jesus—and that because God desires relationship with us.

Lent, then, is our *olah*, an annual offering.

———

"Mortification" is the old word for Lent's devotional and usually seasonal sacrifice. In order to ready themselves spiritually for Good Friday and Easter—to prepare the way of the Lord—the faithful made voluntary sacrifices. Some eschewed the eating of meat, for example.[2] Some gave up sexual activity in a fashion suggested by 1 Corinthians 7:5.

These gestures of self-deprivation aimed to teach the faithful that humans do not live by bread (or steak or chocolate or sex) alone, but by every word that proceeds from the mouth of God. Simultaneously, mortification sensitized the observant to the needs of those whose fasts and sufferings were not voluntary. These twin lessons provided the foundation upon which Christians hoped to build a holy life of loving God and loving neighbor.

In recent times believers have been challenged to "take on" something for Lent: greater political activism or increased hours at the soup kitchen. What better way to observe Lent than by tutoring and mentoring at the local elementary schools, or by helping seniors fill out their tax forms? Gladly, we are seeing throughout the church a reaffirmation of both gestures of Lent: prayer *and* practice, devotion *and* service, are at the heart of renewed and emerging churches.

We do not do any of these things so God will love us more than God already does. In fact, God already loves us completely. Nor do we do these things "in order to be seen," to impress others. No, this is a gift we give to God. We clear away lesser concerns, at least for a while, as if readying the house for a Guest. We make more room in our lives for more of God, and find that there is space in us to love God more. We empty ourselves by faith, ready ourselves to be filled once again by God's grace.

————

Sundays are not properly part of Lent, as they are weekly reminders of the Resurrection. (Hence, we refer to the First Sunday *of* Lent rather than the First Sunday *in* Lent.) But one of the best ways to track Jesus' journey to the Cross is to follow the Gospel readings assigned for the Sundays of Lent. Each year these texts take us from the wilderness after his baptism to the hill called Golgotha. We see shadows gather and deepen as he grapples with the devil and the religious authorities. We see the night falling in the resistance he encounters, not just from his enemies but even from his own disciples. We see darkness. We also catch the first glimmers of Easter light—in a darkened garden and in the welcome he receives from those he came to save.

As we meditate again on these familiar scriptures, we hear the call not only to recognize and confess our own part in the shadows and the shadows in us but also to acknowledge and answer Jesus' call to come into the light.

Thomas R. Steagald

How to Use This Book

This book is intended to help you observe a holy Lent by engaging with the stories of Jesus' last days—especially through "meditating on the scriptures" and "prayer." In Lectionary Year A, the primary reference point for Lenten preaching and liturgy is the Gospel of John. *Shadows, Darkness, and Dawn* explores the major stories of John (Nicodemus, the woman at the well, the man born blind, Lazarus), framed by Matthew's accounts of Jesus' temptations (in week 1) and the story of Palm Sunday and Holy Week.

These "entry points" will enable you not only to see Jesus enter the thickening shadows of conflict and rejection, suffering and death, but also to see yourself in the shadows—and to see the shadows in your own life.

After Ash Wednesday, each week's six meditations focus on the Sunday Gospel reading. The other lectionary texts are listed for your reference. Each day's selection offers an opportunity to meditate on an aspect of that week's story. To conclude each day, you are invited to focus on your own spiritual journey with a question or two under the heading "Reflect." On day seven you are encouraged to rest and reflect on your work, and to pray for yourself and others. These disciplines may deepen your worship experience as well.

See Small Group Guidelines on pages 153–54 if you are going to read this book with a group.

Ash Wednesday

Joel 2:1-2, 12-17   2 Corinthians 5:20*b*–6:10
Psalm 51   Matthew 6:1-6, 16-21

*If somebody comes to me and says, "Teach me to pray," I
say, "Be at this church at nine o'clock on Sunday morning."
That's where you learn how to pray. Of course, prayer is
continued and has alternate forms when you are by yourself.
But the American experience has the order reversed. In the
long history of Christian spirituality, community prayer is
most important, then individual prayer.*

—Eugene Peterson

I am made of dust. I know because I love dusty things. When I was
a boy, I played with dirt. Now that I am an old man, I pray with
ashes.

I was conceived in the darkness. I know because I have always loved
dark places. Even now I am too often content in the lightless little hut
of my soul.

But I also know this: I was gestated in the life-giving water of my
mother's womb. I know because I thirst for the water, the living water
that will bathe me, that will wash all my dust and dirt and darkness
away. I long to be made clean, and I dread it too, for I have been dan-
gerously exposed to the world's idolatrous radiations. Rough brushes

and hoses are required, hard scrubbing, to peel away the poison. There are deep impurities in the ore of my soul, mined as I have been from the broken earth. I desperately need the Refiner's fire, God's purifying heat, to burn the carbons out of my spirit.

That cleansing fire will come (Mal. 3:1-4). I long for and dread the day, but longing is the greater. I know because I am drawn to candle flame and the Light it portends.

All real healing is painful, full of relinquishment and loss. Only death can give life; only darkness, light.

The sanctuary is dark as a womb, silent as a grave. Candles chase the gloom, but shadows threaten to swallow the few who are gathered. The pastor prays:

> Almighty God, you have created us out of the dust of the earth.
> Grant that these ashes may be to us a sign of our mortality and penitence,
>> so that we may remember that only by your gracious gift
>> are we given everlasting life;
> through Jesus Christ our Savior. Amen.[1]

On Ash Wednesday, at the pastor's invitation, I come to the rail and, in sure and certain hope of healing, I acknowledge my brokenness. I confess the darkness, at least as much of it as I can see, in hopes that light will soon dawn. In sure and certain hope of the Resurrection I embrace the Cross.

"Ashes to ashes, dust to dust," the pastor says, smudging my forehead with a cross of palm ash. Particles fall onto my eyelashes. "Repent, and believe the gospel."

If I did not believe, I could not repent. If I could not repent, I could not go on. But already the ash itches. I think to reach up, to wipe it off, but kneeling here I am determined to let the cross, the ashes, do their full work. I will not try to remove them. I will try not to lay down the cross.

The pastor reads from Joel. The ashen cross feels like fire, burning the skin on my forehead. It is torture, not scratching the itch. The ashes are a cruciform coal from the altar, placed on my brain, reminding me that the cross is both delight and burden, ecstasy and agony, life and death, hope and dread, a joy and sometimes a great misery.

The cross is foolishness. It is wisdom. It is our sackcloth. It is our crown.

Embracing the cross is hard; bearing it is harder still. The cross's beams are rough to the touch and burdensome. We never get all the splinters out. The cross is awkward to maneuver through the house and the office, and many days almost seems to work against whoever would carry it. The cross chafes the shoulders, bends the neck—and breaks the heart. No wonder that I want to lay it aside, throw it down, unburden myself of the cross and its demands. Easier to lay aside the weight of the cross than to "lay aside [my] every weight and the sin that clings so closely" (Heb. 12:1).

But choosing the cross means life; choosing life without it means death. Only by entering the darkness can I begin to find the light.

————

The first Friday of every month I go to Belmont Abbey to pray with the Benedictine monks who live and work there. *Ora et labora*— "prayer and work"—that is the motto, the organizing principle, the everyday itinerary at Belmont Abbey and at other monasteries and convents around the world.

Whatever the particular work of a particular cloister, whether raising chickens or harvesting mushrooms, making cheese or champagne—before the monks ever do the first bit of their day's *labora*, after they have done the last bit of it, and many times in the middle of it, there is *ora.* Prayer. Corporate prayer.

They pray together, they work together. They chant the psalms, they go out into the chicken houses or vineyards. They come in to pray, they go out again. They pray. They eat. They rest. They work. They pray. They retire.

In and out all day long, praying and working, *ora et labora,* with a little time here and there for a nap, for private devotion, for study and meals. It sounds—and in reality can be—terribly tedious. It is also wonderfully instructive for us: how constant they are in prayer; how diligent in work. Their prayers are the reason for their work; their work is an outgrowth of their prayers.

Those of us on the outside, the uncloistered, too often see prayer and work as alternatives, so that we must choose. They see prayer and work as bisectors, strong strands to be woven together, threads to hem a day and the years, to snugly knit the life of discipleship. Too busy to pray? Too spiritual to work? We all think that sometimes. Folk like the Benedictines help us think again.

Freedom is the space and opportunity God gives us to do what we will. In that gracious offer we have two options: we can say, "My will be done," or "Thy will be done."

It always comes down to that. C. S. Lewis writes that in every moment, in every decision, either we are turning toward God, and thereby away from our own purposes, or we are turning toward self-interest and consequently away from God's loving will. We give ourselves either to God's reality or to something far less substantial, illusory, and unreal.[2]

———

On Ash Wednesday we take up, take on the cross. We pray. We vow. *Ora et labora.*

Today we begin again, remembering how the prophet Joel, when he foresaw a great calamity on the horizon, said "sanctify a fast; call a solemn assembly; gather the people. Sanctify the congregation" (Joel 2:15-16).

We remember too how Jesus said, "Whoever does not take up the cross and follow me is not worthy of me. Those who find their life will lose it, and those who lose their life for my sake will find it" (Matt. 10:38-39).

And let us not forget how the theologian and martyr Dietrich Bonhoeffer said, "When Christ calls . . . , he bids [us] come and die."[3]

We are called to death, to mortification, to sacrifice. We make vows today, take up little crosses, vow to die a little bit each day, in little ways over the next forty days of Lent, so that we and our congregations might be sanctified. A little. More.

We make vows today, pledge small dyings in hope of greater, holier living, but we do not make them in order to be seen by others. We "sacrifice," not because God requires it, but because we desire the kind of deep intimacy only empty spaces can begin to harbor. Indeed, God has "no delight in sacrifice" (Ps. 51:16), which means to say that God does not love us more when we make sincere offerings, any more than God loves us less when we don't, or when our gestures remain silly or superficial. But when we confess our need for God, our desire for more of God in more of us, when we create for God a space in our heart and routine—"the sacrifice acceptable to God is a broken spirit" (Ps. 51:17)—then God, I believe, is very pleased indeed.

We do all our self-examination with both pride and humility, God knows. We embrace the Lenten journey with relish and repentance, dread and hope. We pray for the ashes to do their horrible, wonderful, painful, healing work, to make of us what God wills: all of what we are, and who, of what we do and don't, by means of the cross.

We pray to be emptied, that we might be filled. We pray to be enhungered, that we might be nourished on that which abides. We pray to die to self, that we might live with God at last.

Reflect

Take time to write down your Lenten vow: something you will deny yourself as a kind of sacrifice; something you will take on as a kind of service. You might put that paper in your Bible, or take it with you to Ash Wednesday services and leave it at the altar.

On the horizontal dial face of Roman-occupied Palestine, circa 30 CE, a cruciform gnomon appears, fixed as if from the foundations of the world and aimed at the true north of God's mercy: a man, arms outstretched in suffering embrace, his face to the sun and glistening, immovable in his filial resolve. But shadows form on the dial, radii from the man to the very edges of the earth; they deepen with each day's passing. Shadows and darkness tell the perennial time: night is coming.

"The light is with you for a little longer," he says to his friends. "Walk while you have the light, lest the darkness overtake you" (RSV). But the darkness does overtake them, and it overtakes us too.

"The ones who walk in darkness do not know where they are going. While you have the light, believe in the light, that you may become children of the light."

Do not stay in the darkness, in other words. Come out of the shadows and into the light. The darkness deepens, but dawn is sure. Which is to say, the shadows tell the times of Lent, but in their own sad way also the hope of Easter's dawn.

Into the Wilderness

Genesis 2:15-17; 3:1-7   Psalm 32

Romans 5:12-19   Matthew 4:1-11

Focus: The Shadow of Temptation

We have fallen into the temptation of separating ministry from spirituality, service from prayer. Our demon says: "We are too busy to pray; we have too many needs to attend to, too many people to respond to, too many wounds to heal. . . ." But to think this way is harmful. . . . Service and prayer can never be separated; they are related to each other as the Yin and Yang of the Japanese Circle.

—Henri J.M. Nouwen

The valley of death's shadows into which Jesus walks stretches between two mountains: the Mount of Transfiguration and the mount outside Jerusalem called Calvary. A third mountain, more of a hill, really—Olivet, with its garden called Gethsemane, where Jesus prayed—is set between them in time.

Jesus' journey to this valley has seen him cross a river, the Jordan, its still waters churning as John baptized the multitudes. He has passed through the wilderness too, as full of beasts and angels as a human heart.

Three mountains, water, and wilderness, a long valley of deepening shadows: such is the topography of Lent, the rugged terrain of our own Lenten journey.

On the first mountain Jesus' glory is revealed in secret to his closest friends, and we too are among those who have both seen and believed the shimmering truth. On the last mountain, his humiliation is seen by almost everyone except his closest friends, but we too are among those who have more than once hidden themselves for the fear and horror of what it might mean.

In between the mountains Jesus takes his stand with sinners, is hurled into the wilderness to stand alone before the Tempter, gathers disciples who soon abandon him, teaches others to pray while he is left to pray—and to suffer and die—alone. He is hailed by the same fickle voices that scream for his death. In abject weakness or absolute power he suffers awful death, just as upon entering the dark valley between the mountains he had embraced the inevitability of it.

The deepest darkness of the valley between the mountains, opening like a maw between Palm Sunday and Good Friday, is still a ways off when we take our first steps to join Jesus in these days of Lent. But we are aware of the shadows even now.

DAY 1 Alone in the Wilderness

The water of Jesus' baptism is still dripping off his chin, and the voice of God still echoes in his ears—"This is my Son, the Beloved; with whom I am well pleased"—when suddenly, at once, immediately, the Spirit launches Jesus, heaves him, catapult-like, out into the wilderness.

Only a moment before, the Spirit had appeared as a dove; now the Spirit is a cutting horse, separating Jesus from everything and everybody that would hinder the moment. Away from the river, away from the crowds, away from city and town, away from Temple and synagogue, away from family and friends, away from everything except the scorpions and scruff grass—now it is just Jesus and the Tempter.

Every year we begin the season of Lent by recalling the temptations of Jesus alone in the wilderness. Why alone? Because alone, away from the distractions, Jesus faced his temptations. That is where the real work begins, for him and for us.

Sometimes we vainly imagine our problem is in the muddle, the mess, the noise and busyness of a day. Too many voices, too many demands—*that* is what's keeping us from the kind of life we believe we would live if we had more time and quiet. If we could just get everything and everybody else *settled*, then *we* would be settled: we would have time for prayer, for service. We could be the kind of Christians we intended to be when first we made our vows.

Except the problem may be more inside than outside. I too blame my lack of faithfulness on external forces, but if I purpose to be alone,

I will be forced to confess a deeper truth: it is not just that I *have* other stuff to do but that I *find* things to do. I create busyness if it is not already there.

We are so practiced in the daily maze, so at home in the briar patch, that *unbusyness* is the real puzzle and thorn. How do we do *nothing*? Or if not nothing, then create space enough for prayer? This mostly unacknowledged spiritual dilemma is both unconfessed and, more gravely, devoutly unassaulted.

Reflect

If you are resistant to being alone, try to imagine why. Pray that when you are alone during Lent, whether by choice or circumstance, you will use that time for spiritual discernment.

DAY 2 <u>Busyness</u>

What is true for each of us is too often true of the church itself. Consecrating a new cathedral in Africa, Rowan Williams, the archbishop of Canterbury, said:

> Many years ago I lived in a town where there was a very active church indeed. Outside this church was an enormous noticeboard. It must have been about 6 ft sq. It seemed every moment of the week was taken up by activity. But I've no doubt indeed it was a very good church and very careful and loving parish. And yet that noticeboard used to worry me and it still does. It seems to me it speaks of an idea of the church which supposes that the church is about *human beings doing things*. When you looked at that church you would have thought, what a lot of things they do there. But I'm still wondering if anyone ever asked, does God do things here? It seemed to be just a slight risk that there was hardly any room in the week for God to find his way in among all these activities.[1] (emphasis added)

We are busy, each of us, and together we all of us are doing various things in our various congregations, but all of that holy activity, church busyness and business, may carry and keep us far from the Holy One. If we are not careful, we will be like Martha in the kitchen—doing so many things *for* Jesus, so we suppose, that we do not have time to be *with* Jesus. We will not be alert to what Jesus is already at work doing for, in and among us—and we may wind up estranged from our brothers and sisters.

In Lent we purpose to come out of the kitchen and sit at the feet of Jesus. We set ourselves space-making disciplines in order that, as the book of Joel says, the nations will not ask of us, "Where is their God?" (2:17).

Where is their God? Are they people of faith or just people of activity? Do they believe in grace or, in spite of what they say, do they really believe in salvation only by work? Where is their God? They surely are busy, but where is their God?

And what of God's *word*?

Reflect

How much of your church time is spent "in the kitchen"? Consider how you might take your place at the feet of Jesus this Lent.

DAY 3 <u>Wilderness</u>

Jesus is alone. Jesus is not *just* alone, however. He has already made room for those he will serve. He has been removed for a season from the people and their demands, but not before he has taken a stand with the people, identified with them, in baptism. Only then was he propelled into the wilderness.

Why into the wilderness?

Wilderness is a term rich in significance in the Jewish tradition and connotes many things at once. It was in the wilderness where God brought the children of Israel after their deliverance from Egypt. It was there that God tended them day by day, gave them water and manna, their daily bread, and protection from their enemies.

It was also in the wilderness where God constituted Israel as a people, set apart to God and God's purposes. The Decalogue, the Ten Commandments, served as the constitution of God's newly freed people. No longer would they consider themselves the property of others, living their lives in fearful servitude. Now they were the people of God, both free and fearless in service to the Almighty alone.

And so it was that in the wilderness Israel learned to depend on God alone—not only for the daily bread provided from God's hand, but also for the eternal words that proceeded from God's mouth. It was there that they tried to begin, at least, always to remember that *only* God was dependable.

But it was also in the wilderness where they began to forget. No sooner had God commanded, "I am the LORD thy God. . . . Thou shalt have no other gods before me. Thou shalt not make unto thee any graven image" (Exod. 20:2-4, KJV), than Aaron, Moses' brother, had fashioned the golden calf and most of Israel danced around the thing and sang songs to it as if they had the idol to thank for their freedom. So it is that *wilderness* also connotes terrible disobedience and the wages of sin; names the times, time after time, when Israel would continue to forget God's trustworthiness and provision.

Generation by generation the prophets would hearken back to the wilderness, would call Israel to those same lessons once more: God alone provides bread. God alone is refuge and strength. God alone is our help in times of trouble. God's word gives life, is life and our way of living: every word that proceeds from the mouth of God: not only those first "ten words," as they are known in Hebrew, ten Hebrew words carved into tablets of solid stone quarried from the craggy peaks of Mount Sinai, but other words too, such as, "Do not put your LORD to the test" (Deut. 6:16), and "One does not live by bread alone" (Deut. 8:3).

These commandments are given to and for the children of Israel, and those who worship Israel's God and serve God's Messiah. They constitute us, and they defend us.

Reflect

Are you in a wilderness? What kind? Are there angels there, or beasts, or both?

Try to name them and their power to aid or hinder your journey.

DAY 4 Formed by Scripture

Discussion of the Ten Commandments—and especially in the public forum—is often hindered by ideological abstractions and generalizations. Even people committed to the "idea" of the Ten Commandments sometimes forget the context in which they were given and, with it, the reason for their existence.

The *story* in which the Decalogue is given is crucial to understanding its *function:* the commandments are not *forensic* speech, abstract laws, or free-floating ordinances but *formational* speech. They not only *say* something but *do* something, and what they do is *craft* a holy people. The commandments are not, therefore, to be carelessly chiseled by self-interested fingers from the quarry of Israel's covenant with God. In sum, these commandments are not *merely* words. Rip them from the fabric of Israel's story, and people may remember them or forget them, may obey them or break them, but in any case diminish their formative purpose.

These commandments of scripture are constitutional: this is who *you* are; this is how *you* walk through the wilderness; this is how *you* are to live together in the new land where I am taking you.

The people had suffered as slaves in Egypt for more than four hundred years. Slavery was all the Israelites had ever known. They knew nothing of freedom. Egypt was the only land they had ever seen, and any land promised to them was a long way from Sinai. On the other side of Pharaoh's watery defeat the Israelites were lost sheep in the desert, a people whose future seemed lost in the past—and so it is no surprise that soon, though they had told God the thing they wanted above all other things was freedom and a future, they decided that the familiar, hard as it was, would be preferable to the unknown. They clamored to return to Egypt.

Leadership experts tell us that when people—individuals, families, groups, churches, nations—don't know what to do, they will do what they know. They will go back to old patterns even if those patterns were destructive, because they know how to do that. Way too often, recovering alcoholics turn back to the bottle when the anxiety of sobriety is too anxious. Couples will refuse counseling and stay in destructive patterns, silence, mistrust, abuse, because the wilderness of real truthtelling is too scary. Political pundits look back to discredited administrations with nostalgic wistfulness.

When the future, the Promised Land, is across the wilderness somewhere, years ahead of us, and we don't know how to begin to walk through the wilderness—we will long for Egypt. We are going somewhere anyway, even if it is in the wrong direction. At least we are *doing* something.

The children of Israel want to go back to Egypt; but God and Moses bring them to Sinai instead. God and Moses bring the ex-slaves to Sinai because, free as they are, they are not yet a nation or a people. At Sinai God forms them as a people, constitutes them as a nation, gives them new identity and purpose—and a way to live through the wilderness and into the Promised Land.

The commandments are for Israel. For those who have been saved by God's power. Odd, then, how in actual practice we tend to think the commandments are for Egypt, for the "Hittites and Amorites," as it were, for the "Philistines"—which is to say, for skeptics and unbelievers. Odd too, how when people and churches display the Decalogue they most often point the signs out toward the traffic, as if to say, "Hey, you! You passing by on the street! Read and do these!"

Only that is not exactly right. Really, the sign should be pointing back toward the house and the church. We need to fix those signs; it is we who need to read and do what we find there. As Saint Paul writes, what has been "written in former days was written for our instruction" (Rom. 15:4). The commandments constitute us, remind us of both God's grace and how we can live faithfully together in that grace. The Ten Words are especially instructive in Lent, all the more as we see how Jesus answers his Tempter by means of the constituting word of scripture.

Reflect

Do you have a "life verse" of scripture, one that can help you remember who and whose you are and why? If not, pray that God might give you one this Lent.

DAY 5 Temptation

Mark's account of the Temptation is spare when compared to the accounts of Matthew and Luke—Jesus "was in the wilderness forty days, tempted by Satan." In that lesser way, however, Mark tells us all more, I think; keeps our imaginations active.

Matthew and Luke tell us that Jesus was tempted specifically: command these stones to be made bread; throw yourself down from the pinnacle of the Temple; save the world by worshiping me. Each temptation related both to Jesus' person and to his mission.

He was hungry, but so were the people. Turning all the stones in the wilderness into bread could feed everyone.

He was God's Son, but proving to the worshipers at the Temple that the angels had charge of him, would not let him dash his foot against a stone (much less splat in the Temple precincts), would be a revelation to the people who longed to see their deliverer.

He would redeem the world, but why not this quick and easy way? He could spare himself all the anguish and pain, could escape the nails and the sword in his side with the bend of a knee.

Tempted. But not finally seduced. Almost persuaded perhaps, but not quite. The world held its breath until Jesus breathed out his resolve: "Not by bread alone. Not by presumption. Not by shortcuts."

Are those the only ways Jesus was tempted? Read Matthew or Luke alone and you could think so.

Read Mark and you do not know what the temptations were, only that they came to him when he was alone and hungry, out in the wilderness where there were no distractions, where it was just Jesus, face-to-face with the Tempter and himself and the beasts and the angels. He was tempted in *all ways* as we are, says the writer of Hebrews, in *every respect* as we are.

Formed by the word and will of God, Jesus met those three temptations we know, and all the others we do not. Surely there were others. When you read Hebrews, when you read Mark, you are left to imagine what all those ways might have been. When you examine yourself, you get a pretty good idea.

I cannot turn bread into stones. I do not even imagine the angels will catch me if I fall. I cannot save the world one way or the other . . . but I am tempted in many other ways. So are we all.

And seduced more than we would like to confess. Persuaded more than we might care to remember.

But not Jesus. He is the one who did not submit. He proves himself less example here than Savior. But example too, when in the wilderness we can remember the word and will of God and keep to that way.

Reflect

Where do you experience temptation? How is that temptation related to the deepest part of who you are?

DAY 6 God's Way and Ours

Psalm 25 offers a plea appropriate to Lent: "Make me to know your ways, O LORD." It sounds like something kids sometimes say to their peers: make me!

The psalmist reveals no temerity. The psalmist's (and our) confession is that we do not yet know the ways of the Lord. We acknowledge that we need to be constituted again as a holy people. We have been in bondage so long we no longer know we are slaves; indeed, though we often live as enslaved people, in the vanity of our imaginations we think we are expressing our freedom!

Jesus, and many of our spiritual forebears, saw the issue of sin less in terms of acts than in terms of attitudes: You may not have killed your brother, but if you are angry at him you are just as guilty as if you did. You may not overeat, but if all you think of is food—craving food, fearing food, using food for comfort—you are indeed guilty of gluttony. You may not have had an affair, but if people are just "things" to you, an opponent to beat, a competitor to crush, an unfortunate to make you feel better about yourself, you are guilty of one form of lust. Or pride. Or greed.

Our spiritual ancestors were far more concerned with sins of heart and mind than they were with sins of hands or feet or other body parts. Acts of the flesh were lesser sins and derivative: done and done. Bad *thoughts*, however, withered the spirit, stunted the work of grace, erupted into bad actions.

They learned this practice from Jesus, who in the Sermon on the Mount was most concerned about his disciples' attitudes. Jesus, of course, spoke to his disciples out of his own wilderness experience: his temptations were less about *what* he would do in his ministry than they were about *why*. Being faithful, in turn, is less about avoiding certain acts than about living a certain way, walking in God's way.

And so we ask God to speak to us again, to give us the divine and defining word, the life-providing bread and the life-sustaining water, for we too are lost in the wilderness and blind in the shadows and caves of our own waywardness.

The psalmist confides: "All the paths of the LORD are steadfast love and faithfulness, for those who keep his covenant and his decrees." These covenantal words are themselves God's paths: not just the roads God would have *us* to follow but the very roads on which God walks.

The Puritans used to say that the goal of the spiritual life was to "put ourselves in God's way," so that God might happen upon us— that we might meet God. The psalmist says that "steadfast love and faithfulness" meet in God: as we continue our journey through the shadows of Lent, that same intersection is where, even in the wilderness, we too may find and be found by God.

Reflect

The way of God is not untraveled. How do you see Jesus showing you a path in and out of the wilderness you may be experiencing?

DAY 7 <u>Rest and Reflect</u>

Glance over your notes for the week. What themes or issues are emerging? Are you making space for God? Pray for the church, for your congregation, for friends, and for yourself.

Called to Be More

Genesis 12:1-4*a*   Psalm 121

Romans 4:1-5, 13-17   John 3:1-17

Focus: The Shadow of Ignorance

Whenever our reading of a biblical passage makes us feel self-righteous we can be sure that we have misread it; whenever our reading of a biblical passage brings home to us the poignant judgment and salvation of God's humility we can be confident we have read it correctly.

—James A. Sanders

The other night, once again, I had "the dream," the very same dream I have had so many times through the years. Every time I dream this dream I wake up in a cold sweat. My heart racing. My chest heaving.

"Night terrors," they are sometimes called, those rest-convulsing moments of raw, unmitigated, sanity-consuming fear in the face of absolute, unmerciful exposure. Whatever is required, you do not have it. You know you do not have it and there is nowhere to run, nowhere to hide. Mark Twain, no less, considered night terrors to be timeless and universal experiences: "In my age, as in my youth, night brings me many a deep remorse. I realize that from the cradle up I have been like the rest of the race—never quite sane in the night."[1]

My particular nightmare dream begins on a beautiful, sunny morning. I am still in college, only it is the final day of finals week of my final semester. I am giddy, euphoric, will finally graduate in just a few more days.

The programs are printed and the invitations long-since sent. My whole family, some of whom I have never met, is flying in for the festivities—I am the first member of the clan to graduate. Mom and Dad are triumphant with their own sense of accomplishment at my achievement. They have already taken many, many snapshots of me on the quad and in my dorm room. They have asked strangers to take many more pictures of me in my shiny robe and mortarboard standing between them, all of us beaming.

The latest bulb pops . . . and a light goes on: to my horror I realize I have to take one more exam, and right now, in order to graduate. Greater horror still: calculus.

But I never took calculus. I have absolutely *no* aptitude in math. Even in my dream, I am in the class because of the registrar's error. I had *meant* to drop the class but forgot to and now there is no escape: I am facing the final without having attended a single session. I have to pass the final to pass the class; I have to pass the class to graduate; I have to graduate to avoid catastrophic humiliation to me, my parents, my family. And I have no clue, no hope.

In a dead panic I abandon my folks on the quad. I run toward my room, robe flapping in the wind, holding my mortarboard tight to my scalp. Somehow I find my never-been-opened textbook, gallop back toward the math building, glancing through it as I do, trying to learn something on the run. The text is written in hieroglyphics. I do not understand even the first symbol, the first example, but now it is time for the test and I have to take it, have to pass it, *have* to graduate. But it is hopeless, hopeless. I am lost.

I slide into the cold chair of my unused desk. The seat is hard as granite, the room chilly as a morgue. I can see my breath. The spectral professor glides over the floor like the Grim Reaper, his black academic gown swirling behind him. He sneers, the exams in his hand as lethal as a scythe. He lays the test facedown on my desk; I turn it over to see what might be the extra-credit questions for Honors Chinese. I feel my heart stop, my blood freeze. I glance up to see that the whole class is staring at me, and then they start to laugh. My chest constricts, my eyes dilate, my jaw unhinges itself in a silent scream . . . and that is when I wake up.

I have heard that the subconscious will not let us die in our dreams, but mine almost does. Another moment or two and I would surely have a heart attack.

Others tell me they have had that same dream—and why do so many of them involve *math*—or if not that one exactly, then another one very much like it: a certified letter arrives from the IRS; you are being audited, but suddenly you realize you have lost your receipts and cannot prove a single deduction. The hard-nosed detective shines the light in your eyes, growls, "Where were you on the night of the twenty-third?" and then you realize you have a bloodstain on your shirt and absolutely no alibi. The bank calls your entire loan—the house, the boat, the cars, the business—and you remember you have $32 in savings. Night terrors.

It may be a stretch, but I wonder if that very kind of helpless exposure and grinding inadequacy are exactly the feelings Nicodemus had that night when he talked to Jesus.

DAY 1 <u>Night</u>

The story is a familiar one, and perhaps too familiar. Though it is one of the crucial stories in John's presentation of the gospel—and every nuance, almost every word, makes a difference—we sometimes race by as we read and hear. Sometimes we imagine we already know what Jesus is saying here and to whom. No one sermon, however, no one lens or interpretation, can do this text justice. John 3:17 is at least as important as John 3:16, but even these, isolated from the rest of the story, lose much of their power. This story gushes, as scholars sometimes describe it, with a "surplus of meaning."

Nicodemus was a ruler or leader of the Jews. He was a Pharisee, himself a teacher and recognized religious authority—and a powerful one too: a member of the Sanhedrin. This leader of the Jews comes to Jesus by night.

Why "by night"? My father, a weekend preacher, believed that the timing was a matter of necessity and respect: Nicodemus's own demanding schedule coupled with an awareness of and deference to Jesus' work, made night the only convenient time for the two to meet and converse. "They were both of them busy," Dad would say, and the fact that Nicodemus was not presumptuous and intrusive—did not demand Jesus meet him at Nicodemus's convenience but instead honored Jesus' obligations—was the first visible trace of his nascent faith. Perhaps.

One of my New Testament professors said that the meeting time indicated Nicodemus's caution. He said that Nicodemus was aware of his duty to the traditions and people of Israel. He did not want to scandalize either one by a hasty or selfish trust in Jesus. Moreover, he was likely worried about his reputation and standing in the community—and what would the other officials, even the common folk, think of *him* if he were discovered conversing with Jesus? Could well be.

Another professor wondered if Nicodemus might have been doing a bit of reconnaissance, trying to get the story straight. If Nicodemus were apprehensive that a visit to Jesus could imply to some a kind of "endorsement" of Jesus, he might have feared that meeting with Jesus could only aggravate the already escalating tensions between Jesus and other Jewish officials. Darkness would be the next best thing to an invisibility cloak.

It is not hard to imagine that Nicodemus maybe approached Jesus by night for any or all these reasons. Indeed, "all of the above" may help answer the question as to why Nicodemus arrived when he did.

Still, in the Gospel of John "night" tells more than time. The Evangelist uses that key word, and also "darkness," as a diagnostic tool—to indicate something deeper and truer to the moment than any clock could show. We catch our first glimpse of this literary device in the prologue where John writes: "In him was life, and the life was the light of all people. The light shines in the darkness, and the darkness did not overcome it" (John 1:4-5). Conversely, when Judas left the Last Supper, "it was night" (John 13:30). For John, "night" is a metaphor as well as a marker, and in his Gospel many people are in the dark.

Reflect

Why do you think many of us are hesitant to approach Jesus openly, and come to him only "by night"?

DAY 2 _We Know?_

When Nicodemus comes to Jesus by night, he says, "Rabbi, we know that you are a teacher who has come from God."

Who's "we"? Other members of the Sanhedrin?

The Sanhedrin, or Council, was made up of seventy persons, half Pharisees and half Sadducees. The Sadducees were priests and therefore in charge of the Temple and its practices. They held that the Pentateuch, the five books of Moses, was unequivocally authoritative. Not surprising that the Sadducees were, to a greater or lesser degree, begrudgingly complicit with the Roman occupiers: their sole motivation seems to have been the protection and preservation of Israel's "Holy Place"—the Temple (John 11:48).

Sadducees were generally suspicious of the Pharisees who were laymen and rabbis—teachers—whose primary identity was nested in the synagogue. Jesus' "custom" of attending synagogue worship (Luke 4:16), his use of the Prophets and "Writings" (books like Esther, Ruth, and Song of Solomon) as well as the Pentateuch to frame his teachings,[2] alongside others addressing him as "Rabbi" may indicate that Jesus had at one time been a Pharisee.

The Sadducees and the Pharisees held to an uneasy truce in the Council. The Roman occupiers were content to let this Council rule on most civil and religious matters, and in many cases that meant enforcing the judgment of the high priest, who was not only the titular head but quite often the real power of the Council.

So does Nicodemus's "we" refer to the Sanhedrin? Not likely, because Nicodemus goes on to say, "We know that you are a teacher who has come from God," and the Sadducees, at least, are already convinced Jesus is nothing but a troublemaker. Quite apart from appealing to texts whose authority they denied, Jesus had attacked the Temple itself—the one offense where the Council had capital authority—when he routed the money changers. His (to their ears) impertinent response when the priests demanded Jesus' credentials to mount such an attack (John 2:19-22) proved only how dangerous this country rabbi might be. No, the Sadducees would not be a part of the "we."

Nor, in fairness, would most of the Pharisees. In other Gospel accounts they are most often Jesus' adversaries. The Pharisees questioned and condemned his interpretation of sabbath, his declarations of forgiveness—even his origin and authority as a teacher and miracle worker (John 9:29). Opposition to Jesus, in fact, was the one thing in which most Pharisees and all Sadducees could find agreement!

It may be that Nicodemus is using "we know" for other Pharisees who were beginning to believe in Jesus: we know also of Joseph of Arimathea's secret faith (John 19:38). What seems far more likely, however, is a truth that "we know" often seeks to hide "*I don't* know."

Nicodemus is a man in crisis, confused. He is "in the dark," cannot puzzle out who Jesus is or what Jesus' words and miracles mean. They must mean *something*—he concedes as much: "No one can do these signs[3] that you do apart from the presence of God"—but Nicodemus, the teacher, cannot grasp the lesson. He cannot make sense of what he sees and hears. Saying, "We know," surely means he does not. His statement is in fact a question. But what is Nicodemus *really* asking when he comes in the dark to Jesus?

Maybe he himself does not know exactly. Call it the "shadow of ignorance," and not all that different from others' reactions to Jesus.

His first and closest disciples once exclaimed, "Who *is* this man?" (Mark 4:41, NLT, emphasis added).

Theirs is a question, Nicodemus's a confusion, known to us too who, though we profess our faith in Jesus, still find ourselves at least somewhat in the dark.

Reflect

How is Jesus increasingly elusive or mysterious to you—or less so—the more you read and know of him? How does your picture of Jesus compare to the image portrayed in your congregation's preaching/teaching?

DAY 3 _We Know_

There is a curious exchange between Jesus and Nicodemus in the middle of this story: "Very truly, I tell you, we speak of what we know and testify to what we have seen; yet you do not receive our testimony" (John 3:11).

John hears theses words coming from Jesus' lips, and early interpreters of scripture identified the "we" and "our" with the members of the Godhead: Father, Son, and Holy Spirit. This particular understanding demands theological contortions, however, and so most recent students of scripture would suggest the sentence reveals a later debate—not so much between Jesus and Nicodemus but between the "we/our" of the early church and the "you" of the synagogue/Council.

It seems clear from other passages of New Testament passages that the first (Jewish) followers of Jesus continued to see and even identify themselves as Jews. They worshiped in the synagogue, went to the Temple to pray, kept kosher.[4] For some, in fact, Jewish identity and the freedom to worship in the synagogue were of such importance that faith in Jesus was secreted away and unspoken (John 12:42). Nor should we forget that the earliest Christian evangelists tried to convert Gentiles to Judaism first—and especially to dietary and sabbath requirements—as a prerequisite to Christian conversion.

The eventual breach between Christians and Jews was traumatic—occasioned, then widened and deepened by the unqualified conversion of many Gentiles to unmediated faith in Jesus. This conversation in

John 3 may indeed represent a vestige of the debate between those "on their way out" and those who were determined to "stay home."

The followers of Jesus believed in him because they heard, trusted, "knew" the freedom-making power and truth of Jesus' words. They were witness to extraordinary things on account of him: resurrection, healing, hope. To some degree or the other, that is still the case; but even from the first, there were those who would not receive or accept such testimony. One way or the other they had already concluded such claims to be fanciful or even heretical, outlandish or irrational.

We see this phenomena—overhear, as it were, this very discussion—again and again in the New Testament. Indeed, we are party to it in our own lives and times. If the best and most powerful witness to the truth of Jesus is the faithful living and dying, the selflessness and sacrifice of faithful Christians, such evidence is not always "admissible" in the court of public opinion.

Or, sadly, even in the church. Though our faith and community are founded on the experience and witness of Jesus' first followers, even believers can find ample reason to reject the testimony of other believers—if only because we think we "know" better than that. Nor is that new with us: in sad fact, we will see a most painful example of this very thing in week four, day five, among Jesus' own chosen.

Reflect

Do you experience the faith of the church to be "unaccepted testimony"? What is the difference between "discerning the spirits" (1 John 4:1) and "not receiving testimony"?

DAY 4 <u>Teacher?</u>

Nicodemus, in the dark, comes with a protest of knowledge that belies the truth. "We know that you are a teacher come from God," he says. A fairer translation may be: "Are you a teacher who has come from God?" for Jesus is not handing on information or preserving the tradition. Jesus speaks and demonstrates authority, but authority comes from God, whose Temple he has attacked. Nicodemus is deeply confused, is in theological and spiritual crisis. What he seems really to be asking is this: who *are* you?

Jesus never directly answers the question, which is one of the reasons C. S. Lewis had no patience with those who call Jesus a "teacher," who say they do not believe Jesus was God among us, but that he was kind of like Socrates—a sage, a wisdom person. From Thomas Jefferson to Oprah, many modern figures and scholars have painted portraits of Jesus with that same basic palette—in that same shade of beige.

In *Mere Christianity*, Lewis says either Jesus is who he says he is, or he is a lunatic.[5] If Jesus believes he is the Messiah and is not, then he's insane—much like the guy in the straitjacket who thinks he's Napoleon—and we had better not trust a thing he says. If, however, he is the Son of God, the Messiah, we had best pay attention to what he says and right now, hard as it can be.

It is Jesus' identity that gives his teaching credibility, Lewis said, and not the other way around. Only if his teaching has divine, which is to say eternal, grounding and authority does the teaching make any sense. The world as it is, warring and acquisitive, neither recognizes nor rewards such aphorisms as "The meek shall inherit the earth," or "The more you give away, the more you have." Cross-bearing is quite the opposite of cross-burning, and sacrificial love quite the contrary of preemptive acts of self-preservation. And yet that is what Jesus calls us to: selflessness, sacrifice, deference.

The signs Jesus performs demonstrate his radical reordering of the world. His is a wisdom born from above, or else it is abortive.

And it remains for those who see the "signs" to come to faith on their own, if indeed they can. But the signs themselves are significant—tell us something of Jesus' authority; and it is his authority that makes him our teacher, not *vice versa*. His answers, and nonanswers, redraw all our boundaries, shuffle all our categories, reduce to ashes all our logic.

Reflect

What is Jesus trying to teach you right now, and how is that teaching hard for you?

DAY 5 <u>Hard Teaching</u>

Nicodemus does not understand what Jesus is saying, in part because he does not understand who Jesus is. But he also does not understand because of the way Jesus speaks to him—Jesus' choice of vocabulary. When Jesus says, "You must be born again" (John 3:7, NIV), the adverb he uses is *anothen,* and *anothen* can in fact mean "again," as in sequence or chronological order: I had that same dream *again* the other night, for the second time. It points to a moment, the one after the other. Born "again," and that is what Nicodemus thinks Jesus has said: *again.*

But *anothen* can also means "in a completely different way"—as when we say, "then *again* . . ." You may have thought one thing, but then again. . . . It points to a process, a journey: gradual understanding, perhaps, increasing insight. John Wesley talked about ongoing, "continual," conversion, as if rebirth is always a possibility, many times, not just once or "again."

Literally, *anothen* means "from the top," "from above." That is why Jesus will go on to explain: not born again, which is to say, not born by water, as if from a natural womb; but born *again,* born *anew,* born in a completely different way, by the power of the Spirit.

Not *anothen*—a second *time,* but *anothen*—in a different *way.*

The wind blows where it will. Life is a gift. So is new life. *Anothen.* Get it? You are a teacher of Israel, Nicodemus, and you don't get it?

Nicodemus came to Jesus at night. He is in the dark. He says he knows, but he knows almost nothing at all. He is a teacher of Israel and does not understand either the weather or the ways of God. He is trying desperately to fit Jesus into his view of things—to fit Jesus into the long line of teachers, prophets, whatever—one more in the sequence.

What he cannot imagine is that Jesus comes *anothen*, in a different way, from above, is something new and different. And how do you think Nicodemus felt, face-to-face with Jesus and absent the first clue? Without hope? Fearful? Exposed?

How then should we feel, reading this text *anothen*?

Most sermons that are preached on this text are, I would speculate, evangelistic in nature. "You must be born *anothen*, again, *again*." The word is offered, sometimes arrogantly, almost always condescendingly, to unbelievers, as challenge and warning to atheists, skeptics, pagans: "You won't go to heaven unless you are born again, so *get born again,*" even though Jesus says being born is something we can't do for ourselves, that it is a gift—first time, every time.

Reflect

What difference does it make in your spiritual journey to think about the new birth as a process instead of a moment?

DAY 6 <u>Finals</u>

Nicodemus holds titles, is credentialed. He is a teacher of Israel—like I am a teacher of the church, I guess. Nicodemus is more important, of course, higher in the pecking order, but not unlike me, either; not unlike any of those who teach church school classes or teach the Bible in other settings.

Nicodemus is a ruler of the Jews—which is to say he is an elected official, an administrative officer: he has responsibilities in the day-to-day operation of the synagogue and Jewish governance—kind of like our trustees, or church council, or any other of our elected officers.

And Nicodemus is a Pharisee—which is to say he is recognized as being a very faithful person. The Pharisees took God's law very seriously, the moral law, parts of the ceremonial law. They went to Temple, they tithed, they worked to make God a part of their everyday lives, and they succeeded.

Three stripes, as it were, on his sleeves. Three stripes and he is in.

Or is it more nearly "three strikes" and he is out? And if he, then we too, for we also wear these stripes on our sleeves. We may not be *as* righteous as the Pharisees, probably—most of us do not tithe our bell peppers—but much like the Pharisees we are likely recognized, and sometimes enjoy being recognized, for our faithfulness, our service, our selflessness and worship, our desire to make God a part of our everyday lives.

Jesus says to *Nicodemus*—not to an atheist, not to an unbeliever, not to a skeptic or a pagan but to a faithful Pharisee, to a ruler of the Jews, to a teacher of Israel—unless *you* are born again, you will not see the kingdom of God.

This text has the power to terrify, for I am the one who so often comes to Jesus and says, "Lord, I know who you are. . . . I know what you mean. . . . I am not like those atheists and unbelievers; I am not like those skeptics and pagans. . . . I know, *we* know who you are." And when I say such a thing, or think such a thing, I only prove that I know nothing at all, that I need my ignorance scattered *anothen* by the sometimes searing light of Jesus. Whenever I imagine that I have Jesus figured out, that is when I prove that I too am in the dark.

I am unprepared for the exam, that is to say. I have missed too many classes, and maybe you have too. I look at this book and it might sometimes be hieroglyphics, advanced Chinese. I do not understand the first thing, can't answer the first question, and the final exam is looming.

There is this other dream I had. But only once. I am in a white room, like a doctor's examining room. I seem to have been there a long time. I realize—though how I know it I do not know—that I am dead, that I am waiting for the Great Physician, for Jesus. I hear footsteps. For a long time. My breath gets shorter, my pulse more rapid. Whatever is required of me, I do not have it; I know I do not have it, and I also know there's nowhere to run to, nowhere to hide. I cannot stand the wait. I am about to scream for fear of what I am sure to hear.

And then he comes through the door. He says nothing, just walks over to me and suddenly I am in his embrace. I realize, though again I do not know how, that I am not dead anymore but alive.

How can this be? That he would love me, a Pharisee, a ruler, a teacher?

Well, God so loved the world . . . the wind blows where it will . . . *anothen*. Get it?

Reflect

How do you find comfort, and where is the *dis*comfort, in believing God's love is a gift for the world?

DAY 7 <u>Rest and Reflect</u>

Glance over your notes for the week. What themes or issues are emerging? Are you making space for God? Pray for the church universal, for your congregation, for friends, and for yourself.

Where Is My Neighbor?

Exodus 17:1-7	Psalm 95
Romans 5:1-11	John 4:5-42

Focus: The Shadow of Isolation

Have mercy upon us, Father in Heaven, for within us is a remembrance no tears can wash away. Upon us lies a load, heavy and grievous: the load of duties unfulfilled, of words unspoken, or spoken untruthfully, idly, unlovingly; of evil thoughts reappearing again and again, even as they were first admitted into the heart; of talents hidden; of days wasted for ever. O cleanse us from all our sins; from those we have not observed and those we have forgotten. Say unto us: Be of good cheer, thy sins are forgiven thee. Say unto us: My grace is sufficient for thee. And bring us from beneath the shadow of our guilt unto our Father's house in peace; through Jesus Christ our Lord.

—James Rankine (1831–1902)

L ent can be a time for us to look away from the center and to the edges, where so many live in the shadow of isolation. We look with compassion, for all of us know what it feels like to be on the edges, how hard it can be to discover, know, or be reminded that we are not a part of the group.

We look to the edges also with this *confession*: we help to isolate others because we ourselves fear isolation. Imagining we are on the inside—wherever that might be, in the company of whomever—we work to maintain our tenuous standing. Shared attitudes, gossip, even certain behaviors fortify the barriers between us and "them." We are all, in other words, complicit.

Lent may be a time, then, to remember how Jesus unfailingly went out of his way to seek and to save those who were on the margins. Tradition regarded the sick, the dying, and the dead as "unclean." Moral and religious condemnations were heaped upon the tax collectors (who were regarded as Roman collaborators), the religiously unobservant, prostitutes, and other "obvious" sinners.

But Jesus received, blessed, ate with, and even commended many of these sinners over against the "upstanding" of the day. He touched, healed, and raised many of the unclean. In sum, he was Light to those who dwelled in the shadows of societal isolation. He regarded those on society's margins as *persons* and treated them as God's own children. He likewise illumined the hypocrisies of the "center" that kept the dark edges dark.

During Lent we may vow to identify and repent of the ways we have helped deepen the shadows—or just hidden our faces from those who dwell there. We may determine to search the dark corners of our families, workplaces, churches, and towns, in hopes of bringing light, revealing the faces of those easily ignored. We may seek ways to go to the margins to find some more of the ones he loved so much—and if we do, we may find Jesus there with them.

If we make such courageous gestures we will be strengthened and guided by remembering the time and ways in which we ourselves, in dark and lonely times, were graciously sought and found by Jesus. His continual coming to us is our abiding invitation to be agents of his merciful seeking in the world.

DAY 1 <u>Mirror Images</u>

"The Woman at the Well" is not preached so often as the text in John 3, where Nicodemus came to Jesus by night. It is, however, just as significant. The two stories are, in fact, a couplet, mirror images of each other, and when you read them side by side you cannot help but notice their many similarities, if also some stark contrasts too.

For instance, while John 3 paints its portrait of Nicodemus in some detail, the Evangelist shares with us almost nothing about "the woman." That she is nameless makes for tedious discussion, but John seems to have designated her this way on purpose: he does not wish us to mistake *this* woman for just *one* woman.

Then there is the matter of gender: Nicodemus was a man; she a woman. If that goes almost without saying, there is a deeper significance to the obvious. Jesus once told a story about a Pharisee who went to the Temple to pray (Luke 18:9-14). The first words out of his mouth were thanks that he was not like other people. More to the point for us is the fact that many Jewish men, and not just Pharisees, thanked God that they were not born women.

Moreover, this woman is a Samaritan, while Nicodemus was a Jew. Hatred between these ethnic groups, like similar animosities before and since, were both legendary and incendiary—not altogether different, if in many ways more intense, than the racial animosities in the United States. Not long ago, African Americans were not allowed to drink from the same water fountains as Caucasians, when segregation in housing, education, even transportation, was the *de facto* law of the land in many places.

And so this story contains elements of perennial forms of segregation: gender and race. There is yet more. Behind the Jews' and the Samaritans' racial repugnance was a third form of prejudice: religious. Jews had no dealings with Samaritans, in part because Jews considered Samaritans pagans and idolaters—not only "half-breeds" in the ethnic sense but heretics and apostates (2 Kings 17:24-41). For their part, Samaritans, like other oppressed peoples, considered themselves both victims of religious persecution and true witnesses, the builders of God's true Temple on Mount Gerizim. Why else would Jews hate them, their reasoning went, except on account of religious jealousy?

Nicodemus, then, is three times a winner, three times an insider. He is a Pharisee, renowned for his religious devotion and sinlessness. He is a ruler of the Jews, an elected and powerful member of the Sanhedrin, influential and connected. And he is a teacher of Israel, whose wisdom and counsel are sought out and trusted.

The woman is once, twice, three times a loser, just as much on the outside as Nicodemus is on the inside, and about as marginalized as it is possible for a human being to be. She is a woman. She is a Samaritan woman. And she is a sinful Samaritan woman besides, married and divorced so many times she doesn't even bother anymore.

That she was ostracized by *other* Samaritan women was the final indignity, pluperfect proof of her status: she is "other." A cipher, almost. Nobody.

Or Everybody.

Reflect

In what ways do you see yourself in the portrait of Nicodemus? in the portrait of the woman at the well?

DAY 2 <u>Do You See This Woman?</u>

Once Jesus went to a dinner party at the home of Simon, a prominent religious leader (Luke 7:36-50). In the middle of the feast a "sinner" crashed the gathering and fell on her knees before Jesus. With no regard to the niceties of societal etiquette, the woman began washing Jesus' feet with her tears, drying them with her hair.

Simon was scandalized but said nothing. Eyebrows raised, lips pursed, he thought to himself, *If this man were a prophet, he would have known who and what kind of woman this is.* If we are left to wonder how Simon himself knows, almost anyone might realize how the woman's unseemly behavior and Jesus' patience in the face of it were an embarrassment both to Simon and to his dinner guests.

Jesus' impatience, if indeed he feels any at all, is toward Simon, who, apart from the dinner invitation itself, has shown Jesus no particular gesture of hospitality since his arrival. Further, Jesus is mindful of Simon's condescending thoughts, and so Jesus tells Simon a parable. There are two debtors, he says, both of whom owe a creditor much, though one of them much more than the other. By the creditor's generosity both are forgiven their debts, but the one whose burden had been greater is all the more elated. Simon gets it, can see Jesus' *point,* which prompts Jesus to ask him pointedly, "Do you see this woman?"

The question is loaded. On the one hand, yes, of course Simon *sees* her: he is looking right at her. On the other hand, no, Simon does not see her at all. He may be looking *at* her, but the surface is as deep as physical sight can reach.

In truth Jesus asks whether Simon has *in*sight—eyes in his heart, so to speak—whether he can look with compassion. Compassion minimizes fault and magnifies need, and such was Jesus' customary lens: Jesus saw beneath the obvious, beyond the woman's sin, status, or situation.

We might well ask ourselves: do we see others *as other,* or as Jesus sees them?

With regard to John 4:5-42, we might well ask, do we see the woman at the well? If we are not careful, we may glance past her too quickly, and that would be unfortunate. We do not want to be like Simon, who *gets* the parable but misses the application right in front of him. Paying attention to the woman at the well may be good practice for looking at others with compassion.

We have only a sketchy outline of the woman at the well. We do her, Jesus, and ourselves a disservice if we simply start coloring in with crimson speculations.

So who is this woman in the shadows?

We do not know her name, of course. We do know something of her living arrangements, but even that may be misleading. Behind and beyond Jesus' comments about her there are questions about her circumstance and story John does not answer. Is that a failing on the Evangelist's part? Or does John perhaps intend us to see this woman as representative of the multitudes who—for one reason or the other, or for many other reasons—have no lasting place, no stability or standing? Surely that is part of it.

Another part may be this: John wants us to see something of ourselves in her. Much as he held up a mirror to us in the person of Nicodemus, he holds up another mirror here. In her isolation we see our own. In her loneliness and vulnerability we may recognize ourselves. To her regret—and she must have felt regret; this cannot be the life she imagined for herself when she was a girl—we can all nod assent.

Nicodemus, the insider; and this woman, the outsider: taken together, they are us.

Reflect

Are you on the inside, the outside, or both? How is Jesus calling you to reach out or come in?

DAY 3 Questions

Why has this woman so often married?

Who knows the reasons behind her circumstance? Maybe she was like Elizabeth Taylor or Judy Garland, marrying and discarding husbands as quickly as one might buy and remove shoes.

Or she could be a victim: her husbands were users, maybe, worthless, casting her aside when they tired of her as husbands sometimes do, the way someone might clean out the bedroom closet.

Maybe she is user and used, both. We can only speculate, and what we decide may have everything to do with our own experience.

What we do know is that at this point she has no proper place of her own and therefore no real security. She depends on the provision of one who has no legal obligation to her. Such extreme vulnerability must have left her fearful.

Neither do we know why she came to the well at midday. She may have been slovenly. Or it could be that she despised the reproach of the other women. Perhaps bitter experience had taught her that she should keep away from proper company. She did not need to be reminded, even by stony silences, how even her presence defiled the social hour, muted the banter that attended drawing time at Jacob's well.

And so she lives in that shadowy, isolated no-place between tenuous provision and obvious condescension. If so, she may find at least some comfort in the breezeless heat of midday when the sun itself is her only adversary. At least she is spared the scorching attentions and withering whispers of her neighbors.

If we are unsure exactly why Nicodemus came to Jesus by night, exactly why the woman came to the well by day, neither do we know why Jesus came to the well—that day or at all—except perhaps just to meet her there, this woman.

Scholars of biblical literature have long noted the similarities between this scene and several episodes in the Hebrew scriptures— when the servant of Isaac meets Rebekah at the well, for instance, or when Jacob first met Rachel. We remember too that Moses, after his exile from Pharaoh's house, met the daughters of Jethro.

I am reminded even more of Jesus' trek to the Jordan where John was preaching a repentance of baptism for the forgiveness of sin. Jesus, though he had no sin for which he needed to repent, went into the water to take his place with those who did. That was a river, and a multitude; this is a well and one woman. But in just the same way Jesus came to the sinners of Israel, he comes to the sinful woman of Samaria, takes his place in her daily place, at the edges of her own community and away from polite society, but not beyond the borders of God's mercy.

Jesus comes to the woman by day, and in broad daylight too. He is not afraid of what people might say, whether his disciples or the townsfolk or anyone else. It is for her, after all, and for others like her, that he does what he does. And so he is sitting there when the disgraced woman arrives.

This could be awkward.

Then again, grace always is.

Reflect

What would it mean for you to take a graceful stand with "outsiders"?

DAY 4 <u>Who Knows?</u>

Nicodemus doesn't get it. He *says* he knows that Jesus is a teacher come from God, but even the way he makes the assertion suggests he knows little or nothing; that, really, he is asking who Jesus might be. He is stumped by *anothen* and more or less cuts off discussion.

The woman, on the other hand, does get it. At least a little. Jesus is playing word games with her too, though she does not realize it at first. In any case she plays along. Their conversation is almost comedic.

"Give me a drink," Jesus says.

"Why are you asking me?" she responds, and you can almost feel the curt edge. She knows men and their lines. She knows Jewish men and their lineage. She is no naïf. This guy is after something.

Jesus says, "If you knew to whom you were talking, *you* would ask *me* and I would give you living water." What she hears at first, though, is "*running* water"—the one Greek adjective means both things.

"You don't even have a bucket!" the woman scoffs. "Where are you going to get any water at all?"

They keep talking, but already the conversation has moved to two levels, and if the woman is in a way as befuddled as Nicodemus—*What are we talking about?* she might have wondered to herself—Jesus leads her beyond surface meanings to deeper truths, gives her a sip of the living water, lets her taste eternal life. And she gets it!

"Give me some more of *that* water!" she exclaims.

The wind blows where it will, but Nicodemus did not feel the slightest breeze, at least not that one night. The living water pools up here and there, and the woman at the well wants as much as Jesus will give her.

But then: "Go call your husband," Jesus says. "Bring him here." Only she cannot. She confesses the last piece of her situation and shame—"I have no husband," she says, and says nothing more. Jesus already knows, of course, and so he names for her the sin and brokenness in her life. Right out loud.

It is a most disconcerting moment. He does not tell her anything she does not already know about herself, of course. But we might well imagine that the truth is so painful, and one way or the other so shameful, she hardly speaks it anymore even to herself. That her situation is common knowledge in town makes it, ironically, all the more a secret. That this stranger knows it too should be the final humiliation. But it is not.

Why? Because Jesus speaks the sad and shameful truth of her life without the least disgust, condescension, or condemnation. There is no reproach in his tone. There will be neither gossip nor silence from him. So what could sound like judgment (if someone else were speaking) instead sounds like mercy: hard truth met by incredible grace. Grace *upon* grace, in fact.

It is a grace that Jesus has come to Samaria at all. And it is a grace that he is talking to the woman, no matter her gender, faults, or failings. That he does not disdain her releases her from resisting him. Jesus knows what she tried to hide. She recognizes what others could not see.

"Sir, I perceive you are a prophet," she says. Well, yes. And no.

But it comes to us as no surprise, really, that later, when their conversation turns to the coming of the Messiah—the woman says, "I know that the Messiah is coming," and Jesus says, "I am he"—she is ready, even eager to believe him. She runs back to town, finds even the ones who have shunned her, and asks, "Can this be the Messiah?"

The way she asks the question tells you she knows it to be so.

Reflect

How have you perhaps experienced judgment as a kind of grace, and grace as a kind of judgment?

DAY 5 <u>Who We Really Are</u>

"He told me everything I ever did," the woman says when she comes back from the well, to the women whose reproach she no longer fears. The truth has set her free, as only truth can.

I wonder: can it be that many Christians have lost the freedom that comes with grace because we have lost the ability to acknowledge our sins and therefore cannot really experience or express our forgiveness? In some quarters, the church has lost its basic language of sin and salvation. We are no longer certain of how to converse about the brokenness that affects us one and all. While many maintain that the last century has been quite arguably the most evil age in human history, even some secular observers have noted that we no longer have a working vocabulary to discuss it. Of late, the historic terms and descriptions of sin are familiar to us primarily as entries on the dessert menu—Chocolate Decadence or Caramel Temptation. The dynamics of sin, meanwhile, whether causes or effects, are iterated in the lesser languages: pathology (or sickness), for example, or forensics and criminal behavior. Each of those languages is important, but none has the depth to express the deeper truths of our individual and communal condition.[1]

The problem seems especially acute of late, but warnings were sounded generations ago—especially in the work of Dietrich Bonhoeffer, who coined the term *cheap grace*:

Cheap grace means grace as a doctrine, a principle. . . . It means forgiveness of sins proclaimed as a general truth. . . . no contrition is required, still less any real desire to be delivered from sin.

Cheap grace is the grace we bestow on ourselves:

> . . . forgiveness without requiring repentance, baptism without church discipline, Communion without confession. . . . Cheap grace is grace without discipleship, grace without the cross, grace without Jesus Christ, living and incarnate.[2]

In our own time, cheap grace seems to be expressed mainly in terms of "acceptance" and "tolerance." All are beautiful in their own way; each and every one is fine just the way he or she is. The problem with this kind of language is that it is demonstrably false. People already know, deep down, that they are flawed, that their lives are full of misdeeds and missed opportunities, that they have fallen short not only of the glory of God but also of their own expectations. We *experience* sin, which is to say we sin and are sinned against—but we have lost a way to talk about it. And if we cannot talk about it, we cannot be freed of the experience or its consequences. The woman is freed precisely because Jesus speaks of sin, but without condemnation.

Reflect

How do you react to the suggestion that we have lost the language of sin and therefore also the language of salvation?

DAY 6 <u>Truth to Tell</u>

In John, chapter 5, Jesus is in Jerusalem for a feast. He comes to a pool of water at the Sheep Gate where, legend had it, an angel would come now and then to stir the water, and whoever was sick and got into the water first would be healed. The blind, the lame, the crippled and ill of the city, many of them, came or were brought to that gate and those waters. They gathered there day after day in hopes of a miracle.

Jesus is drawn to one particular man who lies there among the rest. John tells us that he had been ill for thirty-eight years. This place with the others is long since his place. "Ill" is his identity.

When Jesus sees him he asks, "Do you *want* to be made well?"

It is not so easy a question to answer as we might assume. My own father was sick most of his life, and his sickness was the most any of us knew about him really. So many things he could not do or be because he was sick. So many things we had to do and be because he was so sick. Now, if Jesus had asked my father if he wanted to be made well—healed—he would most likely have said, "Yes! Please! Now!"

But beneath that surface affirmation he might have felt considerable anxiety, and the rest of us too. Because healing changes things—for everybody. Healing "renames" a person or a family, replaces one kind of identity with another. The "sick person" becomes the "one who was healed," and now there are all sorts of new expectations that come with the new name.

And so when Jesus asked the man at the Sheep Gate portico if he wanted to be healed, it was a very real question. He said to Jesus, as he may have said to others and himself again and again, that of course he *wanted* to be healed, but he had no one to help him into the pool when the angel stirred up the water. Being sick, still, was not a failing of character but just a failing of circumstance, of opportunity.

Plausible, maybe even sincere, but he has been in his place for thirty-eight years now and the system works for him. He has some help, just not *that* help. Someone brings him. Someone picks him up again. People around him know how to act, and so does he. Yes, it is unpleasant in a way, but it also very familiar and everyone is free of expectations to the better.

But Jesus said to him, "Stand up, take your mat and walk." Just the way he said it made the man do it. The man was healed. And soon those around him had to find other ways to fill his place, had to craft new identities for themselves too.

I have been wondering what would have happened if, when Jesus asked his question—"Do you want to be made well?"—the man had answered, "Who are you to say I am sick?"

At the well of water in Samaria, Jesus looks at the woman and with a spirit of compassion iterates her condition: "You are a mess." She knows she is a mess. And everyone else knows she is a mess too. That is her long-held identity. What Jesus alone seems to know, however, is the possibility of her forgiveness and healing. His statement implies a question: *Do you want to be other, different, better, healed?* If she drinks the living water, she can be.

Sometimes we are just like Nicodemus, on the inside and sure that we have it made. Other times we are just like the woman, on the outside and completely unmade, isolated, needing what only Jesus can provide—a grace that does not ignore our sin but is greater than our sin. His is a truthful forgiveness: he does not pretend that what we have done or left undone is any different than what it is, but forgives anyway.

That is why she feels, what? Liberated? Saved? So excited she has to tell someone, or everyone? It is grace, and truth, that takes her out of the shadows of isolation.

Such grace can do the same work in and for us. It is grace that can bring us from the shadows of our isolation, and save us from isolating others. It is grace that helps us look to the edges, see there ourselves and our neighbors. We acknowledge the shadows, but we proclaim the Light. That is the Truth that sets us free.

Reflect

Consider your response to this observation: *Everyone believes in sin; the question is whether anyone really believes in forgiveness.*

DAY 7 <u>Rest and Reflect</u>

Glance over your notes for the week. What themes or issues are emerging? Are you making space for God? Pray for the church, for your congregation, for friends, and for yourself.

We Contend against Blood and Flesh

1 Samuel 16:1-13   Psalm 23

Ephesians 5:8-14   John 9:1-41

Focus: The Shadow of Authority

Never question the truth of what you fail to understand.

—L. Frank Baum

Cynicism is often the shame-faced product of inexperience.

—A. J. Liebling

Paul, or one of his disciples, wrote to the disciples in Ephesus contending that our struggle is not against "blood and flesh, but against the rulers, against the authorities, against the cosmic powers of this present darkness" (Eph. 6:12). The verse suggests that discipleship is a cosmic challenge, and is powerful poetry.

The prosaic truth, however, is that in our attempts to be faithful followers of Jesus, we often do find ourselves struggling against flesh and blood—and not least our own. What the author of Ephesians names as "this present darkness" is, at least in part, a darkness present also in us:

not only the inability but also the unwillingness to see or embrace the life-giving work of God in the world.

But Lent calls us to open our eyes and also our ears and arms, to exercise our attentions and affections, to marshal our behaviors and attitudes in pilgrim pursuit of spiritual wholeness and holiness. There is, in fact, no discipleship without discipline, no spiritual maturity without diligence.

Still, as any who have set themselves the task can testify, it is a wrestling match of epic proportions—coming to grips with ourselves. We find we must grapple with the painful truth that most of us are not naturally inclined to either wholeness or holiness.

The healing truth, though, is that we are not without resource. Even now Jesus is kneeling before those who desire to see, spitting on the ground to make mud paste.

DAY 1 A Parable

This story before us—the man born blind—comprises all of John 9 and is, among other things, a parable. It is a healing story too, to be sure. We find pronouncements by Jesus along the way, as well. That said, the story also functions as a parable. We know that for at least the following reasons.

Jesus is present only briefly—at the beginning of the episode and then again at the end. In the first few verses we read how Jesus discovers the man and heals him. In the last few, Jesus finds the man again, solidifies his faith, and offers judgment against the religious authorities. In between those two appearances, however, Jesus "disappears" for twenty-seven verses. All the real conflict in the episode takes place during Jesus' absence as the healed man is left alone to defend his experience in the face of his neighbors' bewilderment and also the stiff interrogations by the religious leaders.

The narrative arc of the story, then, reflects both the *experience* of Christian life and the *eschatology* of Christian preaching. In sum, we believe that Jesus was the Word become flesh; that he "dwelt among us." We also profess, by creed and conviction, that Jesus will "come again to judge the living and the dead." In between *those* two appearances, however—just as we see in this story—Jesus "disappears." As the early Easter doxology in Matthew 28:6 (RSV) sings it, "He is not *here*, for he has risen!"

Since the Ascension and until the Parousia, the Second Coming,[1] all believers find themselves in a situation much like that of the man born blind. We too testify to our experience of Jesus—to the bewilderment of our neighbors—and in some cases have to answer stiff interrogations of doubters and cynics.

Additionally, the man's understanding of Jesus increases over the course of the chapter. He at first calls Jesus a "man." A few verses later he says Jesus is "a prophet." After that he says Jesus is one "from God." His final confession is belief in "the Son of Man," a messianic title. The man's revisiting of his experience and retelling of the story deepens his awareness and strengthens his profession. Meanwhile, the Pharisees refuse to accept the man's testimony and are increasingly blinded.

Our retelling of the stories of Jesus in worship, as well as our recounting of the "healings" we have by grace experienced, allows believers to gain deeper understanding of Jesus. Over time the faithful come to fuller appreciation of Jesus' work and role. Sadly, the disinterest in and even outright rejection of such testimony by some serves only to intensify the dark shadows of their skepticism.

Finally, Jesus' presence and work serve as a kind of judgment, and not only on the Pharisees. When, at the end of the chapter, Jesus pronounces judgment on those who claim they can see but are in fact blind, he condemns all self-righteousness. His own disciples are not exempt, who at the beginning of the chapter were so busy discussing the "theology" of the man's situation that they overlooked both the man's real need and also the power of Jesus to heal him. It might be argued that all religious institutions are often guilty of this same kind of myopia.

Other subplots in the chapter could be mentioned as parabolic: the radical change in the man, which leaves even his neighbors wondering if he is the same person they have heretofore known; the distance the man's healing puts between him and his parents, a reminder that conversion can bring about disruption in "traditional family values"; how only at Jesus' return does our evolving faith become "sight." What is clear, though, is that this text has a "surplus of meaning" and demands a careful and sensitive reading. In effect, this episode invites "those with eyes to see."

Reflect

Read again the quote from James Sanders on page 45. How does his counsel help you see yourself in this chapter?

DAY 2 <u>Who Sinned?</u>

Jesus and his disciples are strolling the streets of Jerusalem when they happen upon a man who has been blind since birth. He is not, however, deaf, though the disciples proceed as if he is: they speak of him in third person, *consider* his condition among themselves, its causes, its effects. With all the sensitivity of a stone they ask Jesus, "Did his parents sin? Did he?" One can almost see them, looking down, rubbing their chins, nodding.

Perhaps the disciples are trying to impress Jesus by offering theological queries. As students sometimes regurgitate snippets of a professor's lecture, to let the teacher know that they really have been paying attention, the Twelve's words suffer from a lack of context and real concern. If, on first reading, these questions sound theological, they are anything but. True, many Jews of that day believed that sickness was a direct result of actual sin ("Did *he* sin?") or original sin ("Did his parents sin?"), but that way of looking at things—then or now—is a dodge: if they can find a way to blame the blind man for his own condition somehow, they need feel no particular burden or alarm. Further, if his blindness is a result of sin, they can feel better about their sense of sight. They are not looking for answers as much as exoneration.

These folks sound very much like the many who look at unfortunate others and say, "There but for the grace of God go I." Such a benediction may sound vaguely theological, even spiritual—and, humanly speaking, an affirmation of solidarity with the observed. Perhaps for some, it is all that. I am thinking in this instance of people in 12-step programs, who acknowledge that, by grace, even more than by their own hard "not today, one day-at-a-time" work, they are not where they used to be. For many pilgrims on the 12-step path, grace alone makes work possible. Others may offer such a statement not as confession but as circumlocution. It gives lip service to grace but in fact reeks of pride and hubris. The benediction's "compassion" more likely expresses self-satisfied judgment and relief: schadenfreude.

Perhaps it is part of our fallen human condition to blame victims for their own sad circumstances, perhaps in the unspoken hope of feeling better about ourselves in the process. Such condescension grants "order" to the universe (things really do make sense), assurance that we are not like that, and the serenity to keep ourselves aloof. "There, but for the grace of God," we say, but what we may actually mean is, "Thank God I am not like that."

Jesus refuses to answer their question, does not seem the least bit interested in theological debate. Instead, he gets on his knees in front of the poor man, spits on the ground, makes some mud, and rubs it on the man's eyes. Whether the disciples see what Jesus is doing or not, soon enough the blind man can see.

Reflect

When has your "compassion" been a kind of condescension? Do you see the sick or suffering as "punished," and the "unpunished" as "righteous" ("I must be living right!")?

DAY 3 <u>Re-creation</u>

Did any in the Jerusalem crowds even notice Jesus on his knees before the blind man, making mud with his spit and smearing that holy goo on his unfortunate eyes? Did the disciples have eyes enough to *see* what they were seeing?

"Blessed are your eyes, for they see, and your ears, for they hear. Truly I tell you, many prophets and righteous people longed to see what you see, . . ." but did they? Or did darkness and oblivion rob them of understanding? If they had had eyes to see, they might have felt they had been transported back in time, to Eden.

Genesis 1 and 2 give us two stories of the Creation or, if you prefer, two versions of the one story. The first is that majestic poem whose meter and verse many of us have known since childhood: "In the beginning, when there was nothing but darkness and void covering the face of the deep, God created the heavens and the earth" (AP).

Later comes the other story, or other part of the story. God kneeled down and scooped up some of that damp, new earth—the rich misty soil of God's good creation. Brow furrowed, forehead beading with sweat, shoulders aching, God carefully patted and rolled and formed the first human.

God's fingerprints were all over Adam, and they are all over us too—have been from the start. God made us with Eden's dirt and almighty sweat, and when God breathed divine breath into the little mud man, there was life as well as light. God put the man in Eden, the garden God planted in the East, to till it and to plant, but Adam would be a lonely soul till God also made Eve.

If there are many who do not detect God's fingerprints on them, their lives, our world, there are many others who do not realize that God rose from that creation moment with *us* in the grain of his palms. The residue of all Eden's children stains God's nails, and God has never been able to wash God's hands of us entirely—not on that first Creation day, not with the water of the Flood either. Later, God's hands evidenced not only dirt and sweat but also blood, which poured from the holes where Roman nails pierced the flesh God's creating Word had become.

Let those with eyes see: Jesus kneels, scoops up dirt, and with the spit of his mouth makes a mud unguent. It is creation we behold in this moment of re-creation as light erupts from the darkness. The man can see. Really see.

I wish Jesus would do that again, even now, for me and for all those who dwell in the shadows of condescension with me. If only he would smear some mud on the eyes of my blind spirit, and on the eyes of his bride. Else, we dwell in shadows deeper than those of Nicodemus and the rest of the Pharisees. The last few verses of this great chapter in John are frightening ones:

Jesus said, "I came into this world for judgment so that those who do not see may see, and those who do see may become blind." Some of the Pharisees near him heard this and said to him, "Surely we are not blind, are we?" Jesus said to them, "If you were blind, you would not have sin. But now that you say, 'We see,' your sin remains" (John 9:39-41).

The Pharisees claimed sight, proving only—like Nicodemus before them—that they were blind. Do we not hear the echoes of that claim in the halls of the church, and also on the streets where with self-satisfied benedictions we regard the poor and the unfortunate?

The blind man, on the other hand, claimed nothing and thereby received healing grace and sight. If only we could really see that.

Reflect

What would it mean for you to see all people as being made in and reflecting the image of God?

DAY 4 <u>What Is the Meaning of This?</u>

We have already suggested that that when people do not know what to do, they will do what they know. That little lens might help interpret everything from the Hebrews' wilderness protestations against Moses ("We want to go back to Egypt!") to the last meeting of many church councils ("That's not the way we do things here").

Similarly, when people do not know "what" went wrong, they will decide in a hurry and with a vengeance "who" went wrong.[2] Such is the shadow of systems—whether the system is a couple, a family, a congregation, a religious *magisterium* like the Pharisees, a nation, or even the complex intrapsychic system that is the self.

When a system comes up against a reality beyond its frame of reference, there is a crisis. The crisis can turn dangerous if the system or its members find and blame scapegoats for their sudden sense of inadequacy. In short, when something goes out of whack, members of the system will whack back, will retreat and retrench. Why? Because any system's best defense against anxiety is *management*; accusation and blame are a system's most lethal weapons.

We see deep anxiety in the story of the man born blind. All the systems present retreat more deeply into shadow on account of it. The neighbors of the blind man are anxious. They cannot decide whether it is the man or "someone like him." Even the man's initial testimony and subsequent protestations do not assuage them. The neighbors cannot be certain and so they remain stuck in their confusion.

The man's parents, likewise, are confused. They try to protect themselves against the harsh cross-examinations of the leaders. They deflect attention from themselves even if it implicates or endangers their son.

The deepest, most uncomfortable anxiety, however, is that of the religious system—expressed by the Jewish leaders. John uses their anxiety to comical effect during the interchanges between the healed man and his inquisitors and in the process fashions a powerful metaphor: these "teachers of Israel" do not understand, cannot see or know what is happening.

The obvious truth is that the man who was blind has been healed, but the healing has, so to speak, overloaded the system's circuits. The religious leaders shut their eyes—or let us say they avert their attentions and focus on what might be considered a secondary matter: Jesus healed the blind man on the sabbath. For them such disregard of the tradition both proves the miracle is not of God and provides cover for their rejection of the blind man, the miracle, and the miracle worker. For John, however, their tack proves another and deeply ironic spiritual truth: Jesus has made the layperson the teacher, while the rabbis are those most in need of educating. There are none so blind, John wants us to realize, as those who cannot—who will not—see.

And so the authorities, as well as the man's family and neighbors, move from "sight" to blindness, while the man himself finds that he is no longer in the dark, is increasingly able to see. In sum, there are none who see so clearly as those whose eyes have been opened.

On the one hand, it is no surprise—and in fact, it is to be expected—that the Pharisees will greet the testimony of the man born blind (and his family) with calculating disbelief. These "disciples of Moses" are most concerned to protect the custom and power of the tradition and institutional establishment. This man's "experience" is beyond the pale, and they will have none of it. It is easy to predict that ultimately the man will be "cast out," excluded from the synagogue, much as his parents feared they too would be.

If that is all we see in this story, however—that the Pharisees were in the dark as to who Jesus was and what it all might mean—we will prove only that our own thinking too is in shadow. Why? Like the Pharisees, we are inclined to reject or dismiss experiences and testimony that we have not shared firsthand. It is hard for any one of us to suspend judgment, *not* to question the truth of what we have not experienced. Pharisees and synagogues are not the only disciples and congregations known to exclude those whose testimony is out of the ordinary.

Reflect

When was the last time you offered testimony that was not received, and why? When have you rejected testimony, and why?

DAY 5 <u>Truth and Consequence</u>

When testimony is received, everyone is enriched. Acts 11 contains the remarkable story of Peter giving witness in Jerusalem to the leaders of the young church. Peter recounts how the Holy Spirit came upon the Gentiles at Cornelius's house in Caesarea. These same leaders had been skeptical about Peter's dealings with non-Jews: "Why did you go to uncircumcised men and eat with them?"

But when Peter told the story, "they were silenced. And they praised God, saying, 'Then God has given even to the Gentiles the repentance that leads to life.'" They received Peter's testimony, in other words, and everyone was enriched—Peter, the leaders of the church, even the Gentiles.

When another's testimony is not received or welcomed, everyone is diminished. Jesus said to Nicodemus, "We speak of what we know and testify to what we have seen; yet you do not receive our testimony" (John 3:11).

Why did "they" not receive it?

When one feels apart from the moment (or experience or insight), when one is at a loss to understand or explain it—when, in other words, one does not know what else to do, one will do what one knows: reject, disregard, dismiss. Such is the case in John 9. By the end of our story, all the key players save Jesus (who remains "off-camera" for most of the chapter) are impoverished, diminished: the Pharisees, the man's parents and neighbors—even the man, in a way.

In one way he is enriched: he can really see, he will soon profess saving faith. At the same time, however, he must surely be wounded since his family and friends are unable to celebrate with him.

We remember in the Easter season how Thomas did not believe the word of his closest spiritual friends. For that reason we know him as a "doubter." But what of those who shared with Thomas the glad word of Jesus' resurrection? Thomas's "doubt" was a dismissal of them and their testimony. His distrust of them must have cut deep.

After the various interrogations were ended, Jesus found the man he had healed. "Do you believe in the Son of Man?" Jesus asked him. The man replied, beginning to see Jesus not just with his eyes but also with his heart, perhaps knowing the answer even before he asked, "And who is he, sir? Tell me, so that I may believe in him."

And when Jesus said, "The one speaking with you is he," the man did not understand all that he heard, but neither did he question the truth of it: "'Lord, I believe.' And he worshiped him."

Reflect

How have you been enriched by the testimony of another? How has another been enriched or strengthened by your testimony?

DAY 6 <u>Let Those with Eyes . . .</u>

Jesus said to his disciples, "Blessed are your eyes, for they see, and your ears, for they hear. Truly I tell you, many prophets and righteous people longed to see what you see, but did not see it, and to hear what you hear, but did not hear it" (Matt. 13:16-17).

When Jesus offers such blessing, I respond with confession: Lord, I do not see. I cannot hear.

And it gets worse. Sometimes what I do hear and see makes a mockery of blessing, and *belief*—like the simple belief of the blind man at the end of John 9—difficult. Very difficult, indeed.

A young man, too young, is struck down by a cancer that seems a family curse almost: his dad and his mom both died before their time and now it will soon be his time, and there is nothing beautiful about it. His new grandbaby will never know him. His children are terrified for him, and for themselves in a few years. There is nothing beautiful about any of that.

A young family, shredded by the infidelity of the mother; another family, cleaved asunder by the infidelity of the father: and the sins of the fathers and the mothers are terribly visited on the heads of the children—if not theologically then relationally, and for how long will the cycle continue? Perhaps to the third or fourth generation, all that confusion and bitterness, anger and hurt bleeding onto other people and relationships. These kinds of wounds do not heal cleanly, not even with the salve of time or counseling. Nothing beautiful about any of that either.

A child dies. A parent loses memory. Soldiers are killed on faraway battlefields, and if sometimes that kind of sacrifice *is* beautiful in its own tragic way—if there *may* be times when wars ennoble a nation or a people—it is not always so. Sometimes the rush to war merely diminishes those who fight, and I speak not only of the battles waged on foreign soil but also of these fierce little wars we fight in the boardrooms and in our bedrooms, in the church parlors and fellowship halls. Such wars diminish us each and all.

There are things worth fighting for, to be sure, but sometimes we fight just to fight. Sometimes we fight because we are in the habit. Sometimes we fight because we have lost memory that our first and final duty as followers of Jesus is to love our enemies, to forgive our debtors as well as those who offend us and trespass against us.

We know, most of us, that we are to bear one another's burdens and thus fulfill the law of Christ, but sometimes we don't even try to do as much as we know. Yes, Christ has called us to love one another as he loved us, but we are often content to let our anger simmer, our grudges smolder. We sing "Let others see Jesus in you," but we do not always try to see Jesus in others. We don't work to see others as Jesus sees them. We just screw our eyes shut to anything or anyone beyond our pride and prejudice because we don't much *want* to see beyond our own prejudice and pride.

Which is to say, if sometimes we *can't* see the other side of things, can't see anything beautiful in the enemy, in the neighbor, in the friend or spouse, other times we just *won't*. There is blind, and then there is *blind*. And sometimes, like the Twelve, we are so busy debating cause and effect—Whose *fault* is this? the man's? his parents'? his wife's? God's?—that we cannot see what we might.

Sometimes, though, by grace, some people and things become more beautiful than any abstract conversation or consideration could have predicted.

The person we once dreaded to see approach becomes, with the passing of time and the sharing of circumstance, a most wonderful friend. The suffering of a faithful loved one gives that person a chance to prove his or her faith, and family and friends an opportunity to demonstrate their love. A terrible change in circumstance that, on the other end of it, seems a God-moment almost, prunes away inconsequentials and liberates the essentials. Fear gives way to trust; loss gives birth to serenity; darkness is backdrop to new light; "blindness" is the preamble to real sight.

And every time, if we are blessed to notice, Jesus is right there, kneeling in front of us, making a paste out of the situation and his own holy spit.

Reflect

How do the words "I once was blind, but now I see" frame your own testimony? Where do you wish you *could* see some beauty or meaning that right now you cannot?

DAY 7 <u>Rest and Reflect</u>

Glance over your notes for the week. What themes or issues are emerging? Are you making space for God? Pray for the church, for your congregation, for friends, and for yourself.

When Friends Are Enemies

Ezekiel 37:1-14

Romans 8:6-11

Psalm 130

John 11:1-45

Focus: The Shadow of Death

The commandments are given for children. The stories for adults.

—Rabbinic saying

The beginning of salvation is to condemn oneself.

—Abba Evagrius

There are the sick, and then there are the sick. If the former fight for wholeness, avail themselves of every aid in the struggle for healing, others settle, content day-by-day to live out—and out of—their infirmity. Every form of refuge has its price, of course, and every form of restoration too. For some, the mat, the blanket, is an affordable haven; not all the sick really desire real healing.

Just so, there are the blind, and then there are the blind. While some rail against the night, strain to capture the least glimpse of movement, color, or meaning, there are many who find comfort in the cocoon of shadow, content to call their darkness light. These shut their eyes, close their minds against any new dawning or unfamiliar glimmer.

There are the dead, and then there are the dead. The story before us has only one of the first—Lazarus—and many more of the second. Some of these—Martha, Mary, even a number of those come from Jerusalem to grieve the sisters' loss—will be in their own way raised as surely as Lazarus, who, though buried, came to life at Jesus' command. But there will be others who remain buried in fear, under the hard slab of refusal, in the darkness of misbelief.

The raising of Lazarus from the dead is the last of Jesus' "signs," as John describes Jesus' miracles, and this event begins the final count-down toward Jesus' crucifixion. Ironic, that Lazarus's resuscitation is, in truth, the death knell for him whose capital offense was bringing others to life.

Still, we should remember, there is life, and then there is life.

DAY 1 Across the Table (1)

A consistent difference between happy marriages and unhappy marriages is this: in unhappy marriages husbands and wives look across the breakfast table and each sees only what the other is not. The husband observes that his wife is not pretty enough or not pretty anymore; is not domestic enough or supportive enough; is not a love goddess or a dance partner. The wife sees only that her husband is not successful enough; is not involved enough with the children; is not sensitive enough to the fact that she is too tired to make love or dance after doing all the rest she is doing; and besides, fatigue has a way of highlighting the wrinkles.

In happy marriages, couples look across the table and what they see is quite different. Yes, age has taken its natural toll on her looks. Yes, he sleeps a bit too much on the couch, and, no, we don't either of us dance as much as we used to. But happy couples find ways to see way past those things, beyond the superficial and sometimes aggravating things. They choose to look deeper. Which is not to say they don't sometimes get frustrated with each other's idiosyncrasies; but most of the time, most moments of most days, what they see is what the other one is, what the other one has been and will be. Each sees the abiding blessing he or she has in the other.

When unhappy couples go to counseling, often the goal of the therapy is a change of perspective. The therapist will try to help each partner to see the other one *that* way, that deeper way: not what the other isn't but what the other one is.

In the happiest marriages, though, husbands and wives will on occasion look at the other and see things that, in all these years, they had never noticed before: a facial expression, a spark of interest, a strength of presence or resolve that . . . *surprises.*

Suddenly, he is not the old shoe he has always been; she is not just the cook and cleaning lady; instead, they are each of them new to the other. Not every day, of course—and constancy is a good thing too—but in the happiest relationships there are surprises now and then, the occasional mystery and new discovery. Fascination remains in play, proof that as well as they know their mate, there is always more to learn. They may not know whether to laugh or cry about these occasional moments of novelty, but either way it is a wonderful realization. They find themselves so very thankful for all they have been through, for all that is left to come.

Reflect

How does this analogy help you interpret your "marriage" to the faith and/or the church? your own marriage, if you are married? your job?

DAY 2 Across the Table (2)

It goes almost without saying that, as we come to John 11:1-45, an all-so-familiar text, there are some believers who are, as it were, unhappily married to the Bible. We look across the table, so to speak, shaking our heads a little: *what was I thinking when I married myself to this book?* We look at these great stories and see only what they are not.

These stories are not modern. They don't even seem truthful, at least in the ways most of us regard truth: as factual, observable, repeatable. But who among us has ever seen such a miracle as this, a dead person raised from the grave days after the funeral?

The stories can raise more questions than they answer, and sometimes the answers offered to us, spiritual bromides and generalities, do not satisfy. We are realists, after all, most of us, in most ways. The platitudes and clichés that fed us when we were younger may yet satisfy some souls, but for pilgrim spirits they have the same nutritional value as cotton candy.

That's all well and good for them, we may think to ourselves, the characters in the story, the folks with sugar on their lips, but it doesn't make us want to get up and dance. Better to read the paper and eat our oatmeal than bother with trying to have more than a superficial conversation with the Bible.

Others, happily, regard the Bible and its stories differently, offer praise for the abiding blessing they have here: solid, if not always unambiguous counsel; a record of shared memory; the promise of God's faithfulness and enough role models—noble, even admirable folk, who lived and died embracing the promises—to get almost anyone through the most difficult of days. These folk give happy thanks for the Psalms and commands, the prayers and petitions, the stories and examples that can buoy the spirit of an individual or family or church, up and over the deepest depths of the world's tides, keep them afloat in the most dangerous of life's rapids.

The happiest of believers, though, I think, are the ones who, as well as they know the Book and these stories, are still surprised now and then. They read, they study, they pray, and all of a sudden they notice something they have never seen before: mystery and wonders and fun. The Book proves to be a *living* word, and whether they laugh or cry at the novelty, either way they are so thankful.

So is there anything new to see here, in the story of Lazarus?

Jesus raised his friend from the dead. Whatever, and another bowl of oatmeal.

Jesus raised his friend from the dead? What a nice story, what a good promise, and what a happy day that is going to be when he calls us forth from death into life, and there is reunion with brothers and sisters and friends. This final form of Jesus' care is an eventual truth, a powerful assurance—and like Martha we know that it will happen on the last day. Jesus does not always come when we first call him, but he will come and I need to remember that: soon and very soon.

But is there anything new here? Something you haven't seen before?

Reflect

Reread John 11:1-45 and make a note of details you have never noticed or heard before. Underline the important parts—and then look at what you did not underline.

DAY 3 <u>You Call This Friendship?</u>

Let's review. Lazarus was ill, and the sisters sent for Jesus: "Come right now, for he whom you love is sick." Jesus said to his disciples, "He's not that sick." His exact words were, "This illness does not lead to death; rather it is for God's glory, so that the Son of God may be glorified through it." So, though the sisters called him urgently, Jesus and his disciples stayed a couple more days where they were. *What?*

Among the most surprising verses of scripture ever penned are John's explanation for Jesus' delay: "Though Jesus loved Martha and her sister and Lazarus, after having heard that Lazarus was ill, he stayed two days longer in the place where he was" (John 11:5-6).

Why?

Later, of course, Jesus and the disciples do go to Bethany, the village where Lazarus and his sisters live, but only after Lazarus has died. In fact, Lazarus has been buried for four days.

One of Lazarus's sisters, Mary—the same one who in just a few days' time will anoint Jesus' feet with expensive perfume and grateful tears, then dry them with her hair—on *this* day she feels no such warmth or affection. She is *furious* with Jesus, who did not even make it for the funeral. She is so sick with grief, so angry at him who she *thought* was her friend whose presence might have made a difference that she cannot make her own tear-stained feet take her out to see him when she hears he has arrived. She stays home she is so mad—cannot face him, will not speak to him.

Martha, on the other hand, charges right out to meet Jesus. She gets in his face—just as she did that other day, a good while ago now, when Jesus came with his disciples to Bethany for dinner with the sisters. Martha had gone into the kitchen to prepare the meal while Mary, apparently disinterested in domestic custom, sat at Jesus' feet, listening to him teach. Martha was most likely embarrassed that her sister would behave so rudely, even scandalously. Women simply did not sit at the feet of rabbis. Martha may have been just as annoyed at Jesus. Yes, he was their friend, but as a rabbi he ought to know better. Add to that, she was doing all the work.

Soon Martha had had enough: with flour on her face and a twist of hair in her eyes she bursts out of the kitchen and screams . . . not at Mary but at Jesus: "Do you not *care* that my sister has left me to do all the work by myself?" (Luke 10:40, emphasis added).

Martha has *never* been afraid to speak her mind or, as she does here, her heart: "Do you not *care*?" she says to him. Her exact words were, "Lord, if you had *been* here my brother would not have died" (emphasis added). She is not complimenting his skills as a healer.

Where *were* you?! That is what she is saying. We *needed* you! We *called* you! Is *this* the way you treat the people you love? The people who love you?

It is a question, I would suggest, or series of questions, that we have all asked. Or want to. Some are afraid to admit it, that they have barked at heaven in such a way or have bitten their tongues so they wouldn't. And so maybe they kept it in, didn't say it out loud, think it impious or irreligious, unfaithful or blasphemous.

To pray in such a way is none of those things, though, and we are not the first to offer such indictments. Part of faith is honesty, and honestly, lots of us, lots of times, in lots of different ways, have said as much to Jesus as Martha says here: Where *were* you?

Reflect

Think of a time when you felt your most urgent prayers went unanswered. Did you react like Mary or Martha? What would you say to Jesus now if you could?

DAY 4 <u>Bold Prayers</u>

Where *are* you? When a loved one lies sick or dying—a child, a sibling, a parent—when a brother kills a brother and his nieces and nephews and their mother besides, we feel the sentiment pound in our chests, throb at our temples, even if we never form the words with our mouths.

Your name means "God with us," but sometimes you are nowhere to be seen or heard or felt. We feel godforsaken. Your name means "Save!" but so many times we feel only lost. You tell us to ask, to seek, to knock; but you don't answer; you hide, you do not open the door. You tell us to cast all our cares upon you because you care about us, but so often, it seems, we carry our own cares, have no one to cast them on. You tell us to come to you when we are weary and heavy-laden—well, here we are, telling you we are weary, laid heavy with worry and fear, and we can't find you. We call for you, beg you to come to us, but you don't show up. Is this the way you treat your friends? Is this the way you would have us treat *our* friends?

What would Jesus do? *Not* show up?

Where *are* you? We *need* you! You say you love us and then you treat us like this? You say you love us, but you don't answer our call, don't answer our prayers, don't heal our sick or raise our dead?

Martha is not the only one in scripture to demand answers, to ask such questions. King David did, as did Saul, and Jesus in the garden of Gethsemane. As did Isaiah and other prophets. God's people have always asked such questions, demanded that God *be* God!

When we pray such prayers, we are saying nothing other than the psalmist who prayed:

> Rouse yourself! Why do you sleep, O Lord?
>> Awake, do not cast us off forever!
> Why do you hide your face?
>> Why do you forget our affliction and oppression?
> For we sink down to the dust;
>> our bodies cling to the ground.
> Rise up, come to our help.
>> Redeem us for the sake of your steadfast love. (Psalm 44:23-26)

"Where are you? Would you get busy already? Do what you have promised to do!" Such prayers are not impertinent. To pray them is no more presumptuous than it was for the Hebrew prophets who said to God things like:

> O that you would tear open the heavens and come down,
> so that the mountains would quake at your presence. . . .
> so that the nations might tremble at your presence! (Isaiah 64:1-2)

Jeremiah quotes God as saying: "The days are surely coming . . . when I will make a new covenant" with my people. It will not be like the old covenant, written on stone, a covenant that they broke. Instead, "I will put my law within them, and I will write it on their hearts." No longer will they stand in harsh judgment over one another, using my word against one another. "They shall all know me, from the least of them to the greatest." I will forgive them all, and their sin will be a thing of the past. (See Jer. 31:31-34.)

So do it already! Rouse thyself! Rend the heavens and come down! Write that law on our hearts. Be our God. Let us be your people. Heal us! Save us! Raise us! Now! Please, Lord, haste!

Reflect

Some spiritual writers have lamented that our prayers are not bold enough. What bold prayer do you need to pray?

DAY 5 <u>Tears of . . .</u>

Martha is *hot*. But every bit as shocking as the boldness of her accusation is this: Jesus is not in the least offended by her rebuke.

Jesus does not answer her every question. Jesus does not defend his absence. He does not satisfy her or our every curiosity. But neither does Jesus walk away when his friends confess their frustration, their bewilderment, their anger and rebuke. When they don't understand him, he understands them—knows that the anger is an expression, a confession, of love and need.

Martha's anger does not prevent his raising Lazarus—or, in another way, her. The implication is clear: our bold prayers and heartfelt questions will not prevent Jesus from doing his work in our lives either—at least not if, like Martha, on the other side of speaking them we prove just as ready to listen.

"Your brother will rise again," Jesus says.

"Yes, of course, I know that he will," she replies—"on the last day." Perhaps she is thinking to herself, *I do not need a theology lesson, Teacher! Besides, this is not the last day; this is* this *day.* That *resurrection is yet to come.*

In truth, the Resurrection has just arrived. Jesus said, "I am the resurrection; I am the life. Those who believe in me will live even though they are dead. Do you believe this?" (AP).

"Yes," Martha says, though we are left to wonder whether, in her anger, grief, and fatigue she had any more idea what Jesus was trying to tell her than Nicodemus did when Jesus said you must be born from *anothen,* or the Samaritan woman did when Jesus said, "I will give you living water," or the blind man in Jerusalem did when Jesus asked him, "Do you believe in the Son of Man?" Like the disciples that day, Martha may just be saying the word, shaking her weary head, repeating what she thought Jesus wanted to hear.

In any case, Martha calls for Mary, and at her word Mary comes, kneels at Jesus' feet. It is a sign of humility, but her words betray her real sentiments: "Lord, *if* you had been here, my brother would not have died." It is the very same thing Martha said to Jesus, as they surely had said it to each other more than once in the last few days.

Mary is not alone when she at last ventures to meet Jesus. Friends of the family—religious leaders, perhaps even officials from Jerusalem—are there as well, and they are all weeping, for the sisters' grief and also for their own. They, in turn, offer their own indictment of Jesus: "Could not he who opened the eyes of the blind man have kept this man from dying?"

Jesus is disturbed in spirit at the sight of them—*deeply moved,* our English translations say, and *troubled*—and one could too quickly surmise that Jesus' compassion is the predicate here: his sensitivity, his love for his friends. He does in fact cry, but only after asking where Lazarus has been buried, and only after the whole crowd of them sets out to show him. The folk from Jerusalem credit his tears to Jesus' love for Lazarus, but over and again these kinds of folk have been mostly dead wrong about why Jesus does whatever it is he does.

The Fourth Evangelist, in fact, offers a different interpretation of Jesus' tears. In all the rest of scripture, the verbs used in verse 33—"deeply moved" and "troubled"—have the connotation of "angry" and "agitated." What if Jesus' tears were not for love and compassion at all, but evidence of Jesus' irritation? Translators who soften those verbs, for theological reasons, may lead us astray: we find ourselves *agreeing with the religious authorities*—"See how he loved him!"—when in fact it may have been for anger and irritation that Jesus cried.

Why has Jesus waited two days to come to Bethany? Perhaps for love of his friends alone, so that he can demonstrate his love more or less in private, without spectacle. Very often, and especially in John, Jesus does his miraculous work in the presence of his friends and disciples (even at the feeding of the thousands, the "action" occurs in a small circle), perhaps because he has time to explain it to them.

What he does not seem so eager to do, even from the start—and why he finally stops doing signs altogether—is to make a show of his work or let his work be heralded as such.

Is this why he waited awhile to go to Bethany? To give the officials and friends of Mary and Martha time to mourn their friend, comfort the sisters, and then leave? If so, then when Jesus got there it would just be he and his disciples, just Mary and Martha. They could tend to Lazarus privately, quietly.

What happened, of course, is that nobody at all had left, for love of the women or observation of an official mourning period. And so, when they came to the place Lazarus was, though Jesus was deeply moved and troubled *again,* still he called for the dead man to come out of the tomb and Lazarus obeyed.

Jesus commanded bystanders too to unbind Lazarus, proving that both life and living are contingent on acts of radical obedience and dependence.

Reflect

What do tears of grief tell us? How can angry or troubled tears be an urging from God?

DAY 6 <u>Until Death Us Do Part</u>

The gift of new life comes at a price. The love and commitment Jesus shows to his friends have grave consequence. Time and again Jesus had withdrawn from the crowds, refused to go about openly or do signs, because his "hour" had not yet come.

Now, however, the countdown begins. The clock is ticking. The bell tolls—but for whom?

Many of those who saw the miracle in Bethany believed. They realized more and better than Nicodemus could have imagined. When he came to Jesus by night, he said, on the evidence of lesser signs than Lazarus, that nobody could do such things as Jesus did unless God was with him. That day in Bethany, the new believers realized that no people could see such things as this unless God was with *them.*

Others, though, immediately discerned dangerous implications, calculated the dark consequences of Jesus' life-giving sign—not theological or spiritual but political: new life for Lazarus could easily mean death to the institutional power and position of the religious authorities.

Worried friends of Jesus' friends brought back the news to Caiaphas, who was high priest that year. With the news, questions: "What are we to do? This man is performing many signs. If we let him go on like this, everyone will believe in him, and the Romans will come and destroy both our holy place and our nation" (John 11:47-48).

Caiaphas convened the Council. He was angry, troubled. He could see what was coming, but he had a plan: he was not about to let the

Temple be destroyed. Therefore, the Romans could not be aroused. That meant the people could not keep seeing such signs and believing. He had to end the signs, which meant he had to put an end to the sign maker.

In any case, Caiaphas and the Council set the clock. Soon it *would* be Jesus' hour—meaning the time of his death—and, from the Fourth Evangelist's perspective, all on account of this life-giving miracle in Bethany becoming public knowledge.

"It is better for you," he said to his colleagues, "to have one man die for the people than to have the whole nation destroyed" (v. 50).

Jesus would have agreed, of course. But for very different reasons.

Reflect

How is Jesus a threat to your way of life and living? the church's life? the life of a nation?

DAY 7 <u>Rest and Reflect</u>

Glance over your notes for the week. What themes or issues are emerging? Are you making space for God? Pray for the church, for your congregation, for friends, and for yourself.

Between Parades

I've often found myself in churches that made more of Mother's Day than Palm Sunday, with little focus given to entering into the passion of Jesus in an intentional and meaningful way as Easter approached. Too many years I've found that I have rushed from Palm Sunday into Easter morning, from palm branches to the empty tomb, without giving my mind and my heart over to thoughtful contemplation of the cross.

—Nancy Guthrie

*It's between the parades that
we don't do so well.
From Sunday to Sunday
we forget our hosannas.
Between parades
the stones will have to shout
    because we don't.*

—Ann Weems

DAY 1, MORNING Descent

Matthew 21:1-11	Psalm 118:19-29
Isaiah 50:4-9*a*	Psalm 31:9-16
Philippians 2:5-11	

Focus: The Shadow of Fear

How quickly joy turns to grief. How quickly wonder is swallowed by horror, celebration by lamentation!

Jesus comes to the city of Jerusalem and there is going to be trouble. He knows it. We know it. And try as we might to avoid it, we will not be able. Try as we wish to forget it, we cannot, and partly because the Gospel writers will not let us. They make us look again and again at the terrifying stories of Jesus' betrayal and arrest, his trials and scourging, his crucifixion, death, and burial.

Till now, each of the Gospel accounts has offered a more or less quick run-up in the ministry of Jesus—as if they are racing ahead, can't wait to tell us about the parade, and what came after. But *now* the story slows to a donkey's crawl. Chapter upon chapter, verse upon verse, the Evangelists show us every dark detail in bright relief. With Jesus, they keep us near the cross. Or try to.

Today is Palm Sunday, and also Passion Sunday: today's little parade is fanfare, prelude, signaling the arrival of the unholy circus we call

Holy Week—whose climax is not three rings but three Roman crosses, stabbed in bloody relief against Jerusalem's skyline, an eclipse of justice so cosmic as to be mirrored in the heavens on a festival Friday afternoon.

With populist fanfare Jesus descends from the Mount of Olives into the valley of the shadows of his death. And we too, following, make our own sharp descent into the maelstrom of the week's intrigue. We find ourselves thrown headlong into the ravenous maw of political expediencies and religious machinations.

Dread narratives fill the next few days.

And that is part of why many of us will not go back to church this week: part of why we read the Passion narrative as a kind of appendix to today's service—so we do not have to think about it again. We would rather not meditate on what happened in between Olivet and Golgotha, in the valley of the shadow of Jesus' death. It is just too hard to read, to hear, to absorb—such a nauseating buffet that few have the stomach for seconds, even, or for thirds. Or more.

And so we push back from the table. We turn away. We close our eyes, many of us, the way we do when approaching a cliff. Besides, we have heard it all before. We already know the story.

Yes, yes, Jesus was betrayed by his friends and falsely accused by his enemies. But let's accentuate the positive. That is what people like us want to do.

Of course, of course, he was beaten by his enemies and crucified by the merciless Romans. But let's eliminate the negative. Let's keep on the sunny side of life, aim our thoughts at springtime and resurrection; let's latch onto the affirmative and not mess with all that mess in between.

It's spring, after all! The trees are in bloom, the grass is greening up, the robins are singing. There is so much to see and hear that is much more pleasant to the senses than the dark pictures and sad stories this week wants to show and tell. Today is a happy day! And we will dress up again next Sunday in our new suits and dresses (and Easter bonnets besides!). From victory unto victory, from party to party, festival to festival. The day, the season, the children and their palm branches are beautiful; why should we stare at the ugly?

Only one reason I can think of: the Gospel writers want us to see it. They want us to see Jesus, want us to see the trouble just up ahead, whether we have stomach for it or not. They want us to see the dark clouds roiling, closing, blinding. And also, here and there, hints of dawn on the other side, faint flickering of true beauty that even the deepest dread darkness cannot extinguish entirely.

It is hard work, the work before us this week. If Jesus' first followers found themselves wishing to go back to the good days before the unpleasantness began or, like us, jumping ahead to the glory they might have imagined lay ahead, like them we have to remain here for a while. For this hour, to this place, this coming trouble—this is where Jesus journeys, and all his disciples, like it or not, must journey with him.

Reflect

Do you want to "stay with the story" this week? Is considering Jesus' suffering a help or a hindrance to your devotion? Why?

DAY 1, EVENING A Strange Little Parade

The last time Matthew showed us Jesus on a donkey, anywhere near Jerusalem, we didn't see *him*, exactly, only the great bulge in his blessed mother's virginal belly as Joseph led them all toward a small village at the far edges of the city's farthest precincts: Bethlehem, ancestral home of David but nothing more.

But this time—did you see? hear? As Jesus came down from the Mount of Olives toward Jerusalem, what did Matthew say he was riding?

"A donkey . . . , and a colt with her." Matthew mounts Jesus on two animals, a mother and its foal. The crowds put their garments on both and Jesus straddles the two. They seesaw him all the way down the hill.

It is a comic picture, if we take time to consider it, and a profoundly tragic one as well. And still it seems appropriate somehow, and not only because today is bipolar, both Palm *and* Passion Sunday. This entire week Jesus is carried along by diverse agendas. He makes his way along uneven paths of mixed emotions. He is bounced back and forth between competing loyalties, pushed and pulled by supporters and detractors, is splayed, finally, on the cross—for divergent reasons.

That other time, Herod the Great, called "Herod the Monstrous" by many of his subjects, was aware of Jesus' near advent. He knew the place, Bethlehem Ephratha, and he knew the approximate time of Jesus' birth: foolish foreign wise men had arrived, told Herod of a telltale star, how the tale the star told was of a coming coup, a regime change, a newly born Jewish king. Herod "was frightened," Matthew understates, "and all Jerusalem with him."

Crazy rulers crazify their subjects. Power-coveting kings use deadly means to crush their would-be replacements. And so, soon after the wise men left with their star charts and birth announcement; after they had offered the Star-child their gold, frankincense, and myrrh; after they had heeded the warning of a dream and returned to their own country another way, Herod and his minions hatched a murderous plot: all the infant boys in the area would die, and did die, for the rulers of this present darkness do not cede power but instead are willing and quick to destroy all opposition.

We can see that dark and ever darker shadow in ourselves too, if writ smaller. All of us, rulers of our own tiny fiefdoms, are loath to relinquish control of whatever we think we control. We are quick to plot, to manipulate, to unsheathe the sharp edges of our tongue or wield the blunt force of our silence—all to maintain our little power.

The Spirit of God, though, is ever at war against the empires of the flesh, whether big political ones or little relational ones. Jesus is an abiding challenge not only to the palaces of potentates but also to the fortified unholiness of each heart. Jesus comes to be king in our lives and of our living; to break down the walls we build one against the other; to shatter our spears and unwheel our chariots. He comes to *make* peace among people inclined to war, whether we are fighting in the far precincts of the world or in the near quarters of our homes, churches, and businesses.

Today we see Jesus on a donkey again—and on the donkey's colt. He is comically, tragically, with humility and difficulty bringing God's message of peace. Once again, though, the *city* is disturbed.

Outside the wall, the common folk have given up their cloaks and taken on palm branches and psalms. They follow before and behind and proclaim Jesus' coming as a prophet, the son of David. They are thrilled at his arrival.

Inside, however, where there are *arrangements* and *understandings,* the religious and political leaders are in *turmoil* at the news of his approach; the Greek word we translate "turmoil" can mean "earthquake."

Jesus' coming shakes to its foundations the Holy City and its unholy associations. For this very hour and purpose he has come to his people: to challenge the false gods of empire and complicity. Jesus' Palm Sunday arrival threatens the powers that be as his birth threatened the madman Herod—and so no surprise that this parade will end at Golgotha. Soon after Jesus' arrival, another murderous plot is set in motion, for the powers and principalities of this world always refuse to go quietly into the night. The self-worshiping religious leaders and the Christ-pretending caesars fight to the death—their own, or others'—make war, kill even the innocent, to keep their version of the peace, suppressing all dissent at the point of a spear or sword.

There is going to be trouble, for on this bright, beautiful Palm Sunday, Jesus is not the only one entering the city. His is not the only parade. Pontius Pilate is coming too: Roman governor of the territory and hates Jerusalem. He comes today, and each year at this time, because it is the beginning of Passover. This religious festival holds real political danger: as the Jews celebrate God's long-ago victory over Pharaoh they could use the festival to put forward another "Moses," in wild hopes of initiating another miracle.

Pilate is there to ensure that no such thing happens. He leads a column of Roman troops to reinforce the small garrison already stationed near the Temple. The empire will enforce the peace, maintain order, quell the least disturbance.

For fear of the empire the religious leaders say to Jesus, "Teacher, order your disciples to stop" (Luke 19:39). Read: *We don't want any trouble with the Romans.*

Jesus replies, "If these were silent, even the stones would shout out" (Luke 19:40). There would be an earthquake, in other words—and that is just what comes on account of Jesus' entry into the city. At the very gates arrives a reordering of the world, a redistribution of power: the high will be brought down, the lowly will be lifted up. No human machination will forestall God's zeal or will.

This is the way of God's peace, and it is a beautiful thing to behold, but only on the other side of awful, dreadful things. There is going to be trouble this week. We will see horrible things, in ourselves and in the world. But try as we might to look away, we must not, for trouble is not all there is going to be.

Reflect

In what ways, or for what reasons, have you found following Jesus *fearful*? How have you managed?

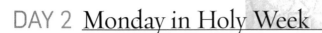

DAY 2 Monday in Holy Week

Isaiah 42:1-9   Psalm 36:5-11
Hebrews 9:11-15   John 2:13-22* (John 12:1-11)

Focus: Spring Cleaning

Jerusalem, Jerusalem, the navel of the universe, said some; while others said it was just as turned in on itself—a little hole full of filth and intrigue, graft and grime.

Jerusalem, Jerusalem, who murders the prophets—and the one hailed as the prophet from Nazareth will be only the latest.

Jerusalem, Jerusalem, who knows not the things that make for peace or the time of her visitation when Jesus comes to her, humbly and riding on a donkey or two, maybe for the first time but certainly for the last.

This visit will not end well. There will be trouble and bloodshed. Just as there was before when Herod the Great sent soldiers to the region of Bethlehem.

When Jesus arrived in the Holy City, full as it was of unholy alliances, according to Matthew's account it was the first time and also the last that Jesus had or would. But not according to John's recollection.

---

* The Gospel text for Monday in Holy Week is John 12:1-11; we will treat this story on Wednesday as a part of that day's lection. The choice to treat John 2:13-22 on this day follows the Synoptic tradition that the cleansing of the Temple occurred on Monday after Palm Sunday.

According to John, Jesus, like most observant Jews, would have been a more or less regular visitor to the city and also the Temple. Jesus had taught there, healed there too, and more than once. He was familiar with the place and its particulars.

In Jesus' time, the Temple represented both God's bountiful provision and Rome's stifling occupation. The archetypal symbol of Jewish freedom, the Temple gradually had become emblematic of the parasitic complicity between the Romans and the Temple authorities. The Romans demanded tribute—protection money. Taxes collected at the Temple were a chief source of the revenue.

The complicity was compounded with idolatry: the money intended for YHWH, King of the universe, blessed be he, wound up in the coffers of Tiberius, self-proclaimed god of all the world. Meanwhile, the religious leaders, concerned above all else to protect the Temple itself, acceded as the increasingly oppressive purpose of the Temple was monetized.

Money-changing was perfectly legal, of course—and a real service, it could always be argued, for those who traveled long distances to worship. But penury had overtaken prayer. Business had swallowed the sacred. And on that Monday, Jesus tore up the place. He cleaned, as it were, God's house.

His actions that day recall other reformers in Jewish history, Kings Hezekiah and Josiah especially. During each of their reigns the Temple had become cluttered with *stuff*—booths, people, furniture, and behaviors that did not belong in God's sanctuary. These "things" were signs of syncretism and idolatry. And though God had commanded that the faithful "have no other gods" before God nor make room for any "graven image" to stand in God's place, gradually the people had cluttered the Temple with unholy things.

We are likewise guilty, of course. The churches we attend, the temple of our hearts, the architecture of our souls—spaces are carved, built, or emptied, to provide a proper venue, a meeting place, for us to experience God: a space for God alone to fill. Gradually, though, we begin to fill in the emptiness with stuff. The stuff may or may not have religious or historic value, sacramental or sacred worth. In any case, such "things" come between us and God, are "before God," shielding us from the terrible and wonderful intimacy that engenders true epiphanies.

Church "work" is one of those buffers, of course. Behind the wall of her kitchen in Bethany, Martha is busy making dinner for Jesus. Her work *for* him keeps her safely away *from* him. Similarly, there is a danger that for those who are busiest for God, many times these things are "before" God—in terms not just of priority but also of proximity. Our works are often a shield against religious experiences, places to hide, self-styled protection against the terror and wonder of real prayer and worship.

On that long-ago Monday, Jesus' actions in the Temple were directed against the priests and the "work" of the Temple, the religious professionals and their helpers, who, like contemporary preachers and their people, may do their religious work as a kind of self-care. Imagining, perhaps vainly, that we are serving God, we may find that, in truth, we are seeking only protection, whether from our creditors or our Creator.

Reflect

What stands "before" God in your spiritual life, not so much as idol—though it could be—but more as a wall, a buffer, a shield against real religious experience?

DAY 3 Tuesday in Holy Week

Isaiah 49:1-7   Psalm 71:1-14
1 Corinthians 1:18-31   John 12:20-36

Focus: Oblivion

There were essentially three crowds casting their shadows around Jesus during Holy Week. The first crowd was made up of the users, those who just wanted something from Jesus, whether a personal miracle or political transformation—consider theirs the shadow of selfishness. These hailed him outside the city on Palm Sunday, wanted him to seize power and, when he achieved it, to spread the wealth. Even some of Jesus' own disciples were in this crowd at one time or the other: James and John had said, "Grant us to sit, one at your right hand and one at your left, when in your glory" (Mark 10:37).

It could be that the Greeks in today's Gospel reading, Gentile God-fearers, perhaps, were seeking audience for that very same reason: to ask something of Jesus, some sign or service. Whatever it was they were asking, Philip's reporting of it told Jesus that the time had come.

Just as the arrival of the Gentile magi signals that the one born King of the Jews was also Savior of the world, these Greeks' request reveals that the one to be crucified as a threat to peace is actually its Prince.

A second crowd around Jesus comprised the abusers. Theirs is the shadow of malevolence. They hated Jesus and his message, wanted him gone and good riddance. Some of them—and perhaps Judas is to be accounted here—may have been believers at the first, following Jesus and welcoming his teaching. By Holy Week, though, they had rejected him, whether for his peaceful, turn-the-other cheek kind of gospel they considered too docile in the face of Roman occupation, or for his uncompromising God-first platform that seemed too radical a message for the current climate and a danger to the political détente. In either case, as the cheers of the Palm Sunday crowd faded, these malevolent voices amped up and won the day.

The third and by far largest of the crowds was made up of those who were—unaware. Dwelling in the shadow of oblivion, they did not attend the parade on Sunday. They were not at the Temple for the "cleansing" or the debates. They were just too busy with life, with children, with work, with stuff, with whatever it was they were busy with, to take much notice at all of anything going on.

A friend concluded his Holy Week sermon by citing the last line of "O Sacred Head, Now Wounded": "Lord, let me never, never outlive my love to thee." He confessed that the phrase had haunted him his "conscious spiritual life," wondering what the hymn writer might have meant, exactly, by that phrase. Was he thinking about death, praying that God would not let him live so long as to grow cold in his religious affections? Or was he acknowledging his place in that third shadow, in that third crowd where most of us find ourselves—so busy with life and its stuff that we are in danger of "outliving" our love to Jesus?

Reflect

In which crowd do you find yourself? In what way does that shadow darken your spiritual path?

DAY 4 <u>Wednesday in Holy Week</u>

Isaiah 50:4-9*a*   Psalm 70

Hebrews 12:1-3   John 13:21-32 (12:1-11)

Focus: Party Favors

Lazarus had been dead but now was alive and eating dinner once again in Bethany where his sisters were giving a party in honor of Jesus. Martha served, as she always seemed to do. And Mary was at Jesus' feet—again—where she always seemed to be. This time, though, she was not his student but his embalmer.

Jesus was alive still, of course, but not for much longer, if only he and maybe Mary seemed to know or sense it. Or perhaps it was with her gift that night the way it sometimes is with ours: we give what we give and we think it means one thing; but when the gift is received, it signifies something else again. It is hard to know, sometimes, about such things.

It is hard to know about people too, and Judas, not least. He was the treasurer, John says, and also a thief. Maybe it was all just as simple as that: that Judas cared only about money, was as cold and heartless as we have been catechized. But here and there are hints, whispers, that maybe there was another side to him.

The Last Supper, for instance: the disciples wondered if, in honor of the feast, Jesus had told Judas to go and give something to the poor.

Which is to say, maybe even the disciples knew of Judas's sympathy for the less fortunate, knew that Jesus would trust him with such a task, that this was not the first time Judas had done such a thing or made such a provision.

There is also this moment in Bethany, when, with Lazarus eating and Martha serving, Mary embarrassed herself for love of the man who had raised her brother from the dead. Judas was scandalized, of course. But was that a sign of his hypocrisy, or of devotion?

No one spoke when Mary took her place at his feet, *in company*. But no self- or tradition-respecting woman would do such a thing. In front of her sister, maybe. Maybe. But in full view of the neighbors? Never.

Taking her hair down in public? No one speaks again, though the air is getting thick. A woman took her hair down only in private and then only as a sign of deep intimacy—a sign that she had "found her man." Which is to say, for Mary to anoint Jesus' feet in this way was as scandalous an act as Jesus' washing his disciples' feet on Maundy Thursday—and perhaps she gave him the idea.

The perfume? Pure nard. Expensive. Used for embalming. In a costly jar that Mary broke as regretlessly as she offered the rest of her scandalous devotion, her heart full to breaking with love and thanks and, also, I suspect, fear—the sense, if not the knowledge exactly, of what was coming.

And Judas could no longer hold his tongue. "Why was this perfume not sold," he asks, "and the money given to the poor?" The Evangelist cries foul, of course, and maybe Judas's statement is simply disingenuous (see John 12:5-6). But what if Judas had overheard and taken to heart the words of Jesus to the rich young man? What if Judas considered those words to be the Rabbi's plain command: that if you have a treasure, *you sell it and give it to the poor* (Luke 18:22)? That *is* the way to be perfect, Jesus had said.

And so Judas may indeed have seen Mary's act not only as waste but also as disobedient disrespect of their honored guest's teaching.

More patiently than he might have, Jesus told Judas to hold his peace, to be still. There is a time for devotion, he explained, just as there is a time for sacrifice. There is a time for *scandalous* devotion, even, which is a different kind of selfless gift.

If anything, Jesus' heart was fuller than Mary's. His heart too would soon be broken for love of his friends, as Mary had broken the alabaster jar for love of him, his grace pouring out onto those he loved. The sweet aroma of his sacrifice still fills the world.

A broken jar, a broken heart, a broken body—each in its own way a scandalous act of unaccountable love and devotion.

But what of Judas? There is the disquieting comfort in the story from later in the week when, at another supper, Jesus says to his closest followers, "One of you will betray me." None of them seems to know who he means, at least not at first. They do not immediately think of Judas but rather ask in turn, "Lord, am I the one?" Whoever it would be, Jesus loved him too, to the end (John 13:1).

It is easy to blame Judas, of course. Perhaps he was just as cold and heartless as we have been taught to believe. What is harder to ask is whether we, each of us, might be the one. Hard to make *that* confession.

Reflect

When have you demonstrated scandalous devotion? Have you ever prayed, "Lord, am I the one?"

DAY 5 Maundy (Holy) Thursday

Exodus 12:1-4 (5-10), 11-14   Psalm 116:1-2, 12-19
1 Corinthians 11:23-26   John 13:1-17, 31*b*-35

Focus: The Shadow of Love

Love is a light but reveals shadows.

God gave all things into Jesus' hands, even the feet of the disciples. The story before us is breathtaking: Jesus, Word of God and Voice of Creation, silently kneeling, all but naked, before his feckless disciples. "Having loved his own," the Evangelist says, "he loved them to the end," and who can even begin to imagine the logic of either clause? But in love he touches them—not just their minds or hearts but also their dusty and increasingly antsy feet, bestows this touch as one last act of love and compassion, of utter devotion and loyalty to them. And he does so in full awareness that their loyalty will fade like mist.

The disciples and the promises they made in the gathering dark—to stay with Jesus, even fight and die with him if it came to that—will disappear into the shadows of Gethsemane, evaporate at the first glint of Roman steel in Temple torchlight. On freshly washed feet they will abandon him. With his Body and Blood still on their tongue they will betray him. His most vocal supporter will deny him, if with a terrible, truthful word: "I do not know the man!" Never did really.

Will he? ever? Will any of them? any of us? ever? someday?

Jesus, the Lord, loves and serves his friends in this almost-too-much-to-take-in way. And then Jesus gives them this almost-too-much-to-give-out commandment, a new commandment and mandate (and thus, *mandatum,* Latin for "commandment" and *Maundy* Thursday)—that *they love one another* just *as he has loved them.* Not only the way he had *just* loved them but in all the ways Jesus had loved them and did, from the beginning to the end. One could spend a life, a ministry, an academic career trying to plumb the content and ethical implications of Jesus' last command.

God gave all things into Jesus' hands, even the feet of the disciples. And he left this word: "I have set you an example. . . . If you know these things, you are blessed if you do them" (John 13:17).

Primitive Baptists and the Brethren, among others, practice foot washing. We might wish the rest of us would. The practice meets the requirements, after all: it was instituted by Jesus, and it does convey grace.

Still, the grace foot washing conveys can be overwhelming—too much grace, if there is such a thing. Light can blind eyes accustomed to the shadows. It comes as no surprise when foot-washing services are poorly attended, when even the most faithful say, with their words or their absence, "You shall never touch my feet."

It is no surprise when even the faithful keep their distance—keep their feet, their hands, their hearts and minds mostly to themselves. Hide in the shadows of resistance. Putting ourselves in Jesus' hands changes things, changes us. Easier to be who we are, even if it is in the dark.

"Unless I wash you, you have no share in me," Jesus says, and we know at once that distance is not an option in discipleship. We have to come close, have to let him have his way with us, have to let him bathe us, and not only our feet.

Reflect

How is the love of Jesus, and of the church, *uncomfortable* for you? Do you wish for such intimacy, with Jesus and others, as Jesus desires? How do you imagine such intimacy would look day to day?

DAY 6 <u>Good Friday</u>

Isaiah 52:13–53:12   Psalm 22
Hebrews 10:16-25   John 18:1–19:42

Focus: The Shadow of Silence, Suffering, and Death

Friday has dawned, but it is still night, the darkness and the shadows growing all the deeper as the sun makes its way toward noon. After their final supper together, Jesus and eleven of his disciples had gone to dark Gethsemane, where the moon and the last of the stars were extinguished by the betrayal of the other disciple. Judas had left the table, taking himself on freshly washed feet to meet a contingent of Roman soldiers and Temple guards. Their torches brought garish light to the garden; wild, misshapen shadows marched to where Judas said Jesus would be. There was sacrament on Judas's breath when he kissed Jesus—a kiss of identification, and death. (All the Gospels but John record the kiss. John simply says that Judas was with the arresting party.)

A fevered skirmish between the sleepy disciples and the high priest's posse was quickly quelled by Jesus, the peacemaker, who also mended the wounded ear of Malchus. Then, Jesus surrendered himself while the disciples fled.

Alone except for his arresters, Jesus was taken to Annas, the father-in-law of the high priest Caiaphas. Peter, who had followed at a distance, found himself also being interrogated. As Jesus was questioned by Annas, Peter was scrutinized by the maid. "Are you not one of them?" Others questioned him too, three times asked Peter if he were not one of the disciples, but each time Peter said, "I am not." The cock crowed after the third denial, but not to greet the day.

Inside, Jesus' interrogation turned nasty when, upon answering one of Annas's questions, he was struck in the face by one of the policemen. "If I have spoken wrongly, testify to the wrong," Jesus said. "But if I have spoken rightly, why do you strike me?" Perhaps, then as now, he was struck precisely because he does speak the truth. Jesus was bound and carted off to Caiaphas.

After a brief visit to the high priest himself, Jesus was taken to Pilate, the Roman governor. Pilate seems pitiable—almost: an inquisitor defending himself to the Judge. It is Pilate who is on trial, not Jesus. But when Pilate found no reason to charge, much less hold, Jesus, the will of the crowd rendered Pilate powerless yet again: he could not protect Jesus. The crowd demanded Barabbas's release, and it was granted. They demanded Jesus' death, and Pilate recused himself, acceded to their wishes. Jesus was flogged, mocked, condemned to death.

About noon, while lambs were being slaughtered at the Temple for the Passover meal, Jesus was stripped, nailed to a cross, and put on hideous display for anyone passing by to see. Defying the crowds at last, Pilate commissioned a sign to be hung on the cross: "The King of the Jews." It was written in three languages, so that no one missed it. But what did Pilate mean? This is what we do to troublemakers? Or did he maybe believe it himself?

Soon it was over, finished. Jesus died in only three hours, but he continued his earthly work even to the end. With almost his last breath he did what he always did: reordered lives and relationships. "Here is your son," he said to Mary, indicating the disciple he loved. And to him in turn, Jesus said, "Here is your mother." That was Jesus' ministry from the very start—giving his followers to one another in new ways.

It is to this precise moment that everything prior has led. And we would turn away from it, partly because we know the story so well and partly because we really haven't the first clue as to what it all means. How does *this* death, this *death*, bring life?

Many have tried to put words around it, bring sense to it or purpose out of it. Better, perhaps, to fall silent. Or turn to the Psalms. Jesus used a few of his last breaths to quote the beginning of Psalm 22, as a way to interpret his own experience of that moment—though only Matthew and Mark have the stomach to remember that he did.

Maybe we turn to another psalm, not to interpret Jesus' death so much as to understand the nature of our own lives.

> LORD, let me know my end,
>   and what is the measure of my days;
>   let me know how fleeting my life is.
> You have made my days a few handbreadths,
>   and my lifetime is as nothing in your sight.
> Surely everyone stands as a mere breath.
> Surely everyone goes about like a shadow.
> Surely for nothing they are in turmoil;
>   they heap up, and do not know who will gather.
>
> And now, O Lord, what do I wait for?
>   My hope is in you.
>
>   .   .   .   .   .   .
>
> Hear my prayer, O LORD,
>   and give ear to my cry;
>   do not hold your peace at my tears. (Psalm 39:4-7, 12*a*)

Reflect

How do you respond to this frequently quoted statement: *A faith unequal to death is a faith also unequal to life*? Do you see our culture as death-denying? How might "knowing our end" and "dying well" be prophetic testimony to our culture?

DAY 7 <u>Holy Saturday</u>

Be still today. Glance over your notes for the week. What themes or issues are emerging? Are you making space for God? Pray for the church, for your congregation, for friends, and for yourself.

Easter Vigil/Easter Day

Light in the Darkness

| Acts 10:34-43 | Psalm 118:1-2, 14-24 |
| Colossians 3:1-4 | John 20:1-18, (19-29) |

Focus: The Light Shines in Darkness

Who knows in what partial way the long expected one appears, in what disguise the one who is to come comes.

—Frederick Buechner

I f the Light were eclipsed by the horrors of Friday afternoon, by Sunday morning the darkness was already passing away, the true light already shining—though none even among his followers could yet see it or know. Easter's miracle was swaddled in nighttime, and perhaps for mercy's sake: eyes and minds grown accustomed to the shadows instinctively defend themselves against the dawn.

Before sunrise on Sunday, the first day of the week, while it was yet dark, one or a few of the women who followed Jesus made their way to the tomb garden, thinking only to attend to his ruined body. The men came to the tomb only later, and then only a couple of them and somewhat reluctantly.

Long centuries later, a collection of chilly souls, some of them just as reluctant and all of them bundled, sleepy, and shivering, gather a few minutes before midnight in a large cemetery about a stone's throw from the small aluminum-sided sanctuary. Time and familiarity have not diminished the near-comedy of this ritual—the Easter Vigil.

The dead far outnumber the quick, and the darkness takes scant notice of the solitary candle around which we cluster. An early spring breeze glides through the still-mostly-bare branches of trees warding the sacred acre. The flame dances, or teeters, flickers and more than once all but goes out. Soon we will make our pilgrim way along the long concrete walkway from cemetery to sanctuary— from the darkness into light, from the memory of death into hope for new life.

The assembled few represent the absent many—all of us simultaneously shackled to yesterday and straining toward tomorrow. "Night" describes not only the time of day but also the condition of our souls. We stand here half from habit, half in hungering hope, the latter often unrecognized and certainly unconfessed. Yes, we believe what we are about to proclaim—Alleluia! Christ is risen!—but Lord, help our unbelief.

If the Lord is risen indeed, it changes everything, but most days it seems as if nothing, not even our own lives, is very much different since last Easter, or in all the Easters since those first few souls made their way to the cemetery outside the gates of Jerusalem. We want to believe—do believe—that the night is passing away, that the light is already dawning. But in just an hour's time we will leave this first celebration of Easter and, as if living a parable, look for our cars in the parking lot by the glow of a distant streetlamp. Yes, indeed, Christ is risen, but this spring night/morning is even darker than it was when we arrived and we ourselves are sleepier than we were, scriptures and hymns and the Exsultet notwithstanding. What has changed *really* on account of our proclamation? The rabbis used to debate, feverishly, why the Lord God, blessed be he, King of the universe, used such a puny miracle to summon Moses into his service. A bush? A burning *bush*? Eventually the rabbis determined that the bush was *no* miracle at all. Instead, the bush was a test, a tool to ascertain Moses' powers of observation.

Would Moses *notice* God's handiwork in the world if he came across it? Would he be alert enough to see things out of the *ordinary*? Would Moses, like most shepherds, be so focused on the dangers of the wilderness that he would overlook mystery? Would Moses have eyes to *see* a bush that burned, to *notice* the bush was not consumed?

He did, of course, and the rest is salvation history.

Observation—really seeing what is there—has been a crucial part of the spiritual life ever since. Remember how often Jesus said, "Let those with eyes to see, see"? God planted the bush for Moses while Jesus told the parables for his disciples—as a kind of test: he wanted his followers to see beyond the obvious, beneath the surface.

The fiery presence of God flames up in unlikely places, he seemed to be teaching: light emerges in shadows and so we remain attentive and alert. The cold folly of our sinful condition is also apparent, crops up everywhere, but many do not want to see or acknowledge either glory or sin. To see either demands courage, hope, and the capacity to laugh, and to cry.

Being a disciple means we listen too—"let those with ears, hear"— and speak, even when others disregard our witness.

———

Jesus said to Nicodemus, "We speak of what we know and testify to what we have seen; yet you do not receive our testimony" (John 3:11). To whom is Jesus referring? Who does not receive testimony? Even his own disciples, of course.

It is no surprise, then, that our Easter-evening attentions are focused on Thomas—called "the Twin" by John, and in fact a twin to any and all who demand "proof" or explanation of the Resurrection. He is twin to all of us, in other words, at one time or another. Indeed, I suspect the Fourth Evangelist hoped to suggest such a sibling relationship between Thomas and every believer. As regards Easter itself, however, I find that Thomas and I are *inversely* related. My need, in other words, is the opposite of Thomas's.

Thomas demanded to touch Jesus' ruined hands before he would believe that the Crucified had been raised. He said he would not believe unless he could put his hand in the wound in Jesus' side. He needed to see for himself, thank you very much, before he would believe the testimony he had heard.

His demands show what Thomas thought of the other disciples: he considered them untrustworthy, unbelievable, in fact.

But what, I wonder, did the other disciples think of Thomas? We can only imagine. Or can you remember a situation when someone who should have trusted you did not? You told them something, this or that, and they did not blink or nod, did not smile, more like smirked when they said, simply and dismissively, "Well, I will have to see *that* for myself."

I do not respond well to such dismissals, and especially when I share the good news with people, confide in them my deepest beliefs and commitments. If they reject my testimony out of hand, that means they do not trust that I am telling them the truth. When that happens, I feel my breath get a bit shallow, my mouth a bit dry. I sometimes feel my hands clinching into a nascent fist (not that I would ever use them; I am much too much a coward for that). My heart hardens.

That is why I so desperately need the mirror image of what Thomas demanded: I need Jesus to touch my hands, to unfist them. I need Jesus to reach into my chest and massage, soften, my hard heart. If I am going to keep sharing this good news with folk, and if they are going to continue disregarding me, not trusting me, humoring me or even just ignoring me—it is going to take a touch of Jesus for me to keep at it.

The light shines in the darkness. We believe and proclaim that the shadows in the world and in our hearts are dispelled by the Day. And so may God grant us to see the moments and the lives that burn with Easter fire. And may God grant us the Spirit to bear witness to what we see and have heard, even when others do not believe.

Reflect for the Great Fifty Days (the Easter Season)

Some say Easter is the heart of Christian timekeeping and that every Sunday is a "little Easter." Some say that Sunday is the heart of Christian timekeeping and that Easter is the "big Sunday." How do these two perspectives shape us in different ways?

Where have you noticed "proof" of the Resurrection—light that only God could provide in our dark world? What keeps you from noticing the "burning bushes" God may have placed within plain sight? Consider an Easter vow to "be alert" as a follow-up to your Lenten vow.

Afterword

May the mind of Christ, my Savior,
Live in me from day to day,
By His love and power controlling
All I do and say.

May the Word of God dwell richly
In my heart from hour to hour,
So that all may see I triumph
Only through His power.

May the peace of God my Father
Rule my life in everything,
That I may be calm to comfort
Sick and sorrowing.

May the love of Jesus fill me
As the waters fill the sea;
Him exalting, self abasing,
This is victory.

May I run the race before me,
Strong and brave to face the foe,
Looking only unto Jesus
As I onward go.

May His beauty rest upon me,
As I seek the lost to win,
And may they forget the channel,
Seeing only Him.

—Kate B. Wilkinson, 1925

Small Group Guidelines

Here is a simple plan for a weekly gathering during Lent to talk about *Shadows, Darkness, and Dawn*. One person may act as convener every week, or the role can rotate among group members. You may want to light a white Christ candle each week to signal the beginning of your time together.

Opening

Convener: Let us come into the presence of God.

Others: Lord Jesus Christ, thank you for being with us. May we hear your word to us as we speak to one another.

Scripture

Convener reads the Sunday gospel for the week. After a one- or two-minute silence, convener asks: What did you hear God saying to you in this passage? What response does this call for? (Group members respond in turn or as led.)

Reflection

• What meditation(s) from this week was (were) particularly meaningful for you? Why? (Group members respond in turn or as led.)

• How have you experienced God's grace this week? Have you been able to love God more?

• In what ways have the readings challenged you? How has your prayer life been affected?

- Comment on the "Reflect" questions that particularly deepened your own self-examination and practice.

Praying together

Convener: Based on today's conversation, what people and situations do you want us to pray for now and in the coming week?

Convener or other volunteer then prays about the concerns named.

Closing

Convener: Let us go in peace to serve God and our neighbors in all that we do.

Adapted from *The Upper Room* daily devotional guide, January–February 2001. © 2000 The Upper Room. Used by permission.

Epigraph Sources

Introduction

Kathleen Norris, *Acedia and Me: A Marriage, Monks, and a Writer's Life* (New York: Riverhead Books, 2008), 132.

Ash Wednesday

Eugene Peterson, *The Contemplative Pastor: Returning to the Art of Spiritual Direction* (Grand Rapids, MI: Eerdmans, 1989), 8.

Week One

Henri J. M. Nouwen, *The Living Reminder: Service and Prayer in Memory of Jesus Christ* (New York: Seabury Press, 1977), 12–13.

Week Two

James A. Sanders, *God Has a Story Too* (Minneapolis, MN: Fortress Press, 1979), 48.

Week Three

James Rankine, cited in John Birkbeck, ed., *A Private Devotional Diary* (Atlanta: John Knox, 1975), 52.

Week Four

L. Frank Baum, *Rinkitink in Oz*, http://www.gutenberg.org/etexts/958.

A. J. Liebling, "Quest for Mollie," in *Just Enough Liebling* (New York: North Point Press/Farrar, Straus, 2004), 177.

Week Five

Abba Evagrius, quoted in *The Orthodox Way* by Bishop Kallistos Ware (Crestwood: St. Vladimir's Seminary Press, 1999), 113.

Week Six

Nancy Guthrie, ed., *Jesus, Keep Me Near the Cross: Experiencing the Passion and Power of Easter* (Wheaton, IL: Crossway Books, 2009), 9.

Ann Weems, *Kneeling in Jerusalem* (Westminster/John Knox Press, 1992), 69.

Easter

Frederick Buechner, *The Alphabet of Grace* (New York: HarperCollins, 1989), 103.

Notes

Introduction

1. These are the traditional practices of Lent, enumerated in the "Invitation to a Holy Lent" as found, for example, in *The United Methodist Book of Worship* and the Book of Common Prayer.

2. Fasting is not only about food. It can be, but there are other forms. Maybe we turn off the TV for an hour a day and spend that time reading our Bibles, praying, or even playing a board game with our kids or grandkids. Maybe we give up our cell phones, at least during meals out with the family, or determine to check our e-mail and RSS feeds only once a day.

Ash Wednesday

1. *The United Methodist Book of Worship*, 323.

2. See C. S. Lewis, *Mere Christianity*, rev. ed. (New York: Collier Books, 1960), 86–89.

3. Dietrich Bonhoeffer, *The Cost of Discipleship*, rev. ed., trans. R. H. Fuller, with some revision by Irmgard Booth (New York: Collier Books, 1963), 99.

Week One

1. http://timescolumns.typepad.com/gledhill/2009/02/archbishop-of-canterbury-churches

Week Two

1. Charles Neider, ed., *The Autobiography of Mark Twain* (New York: Perennial Classics/ Harper and Row, 1959), 46.

2. The Pharisees accepted the Prophets and the Writings as authoritative, as well as the books of Moses. In contrast to the Sadducees, however, who were most concerned with the "ceremonial" aspects of the Pentateuch (the details of Temple worship), the Pharisees were more concerned with the "ethical" aspects of Israel's history, the same emphases they found in the Prophets and the Writings.

3. *Signs* is John's characteristic word for what might otherwise be called a miracle, for in John these powerful acts show us something of who Jesus is, the Incarnate Word, and therefore something of who God is. Jesus speaks, as God spoke at Creation, and things happen.

4. See respectively, among other passages, Acts 3:1; 10:14; 13:13-46.

5. Lewis, *Mere Christianity*, 56.

Week Three

1. See Barbara Brown Taylor, *Speaking of Sin: The Lost Language of Salvation* (Cambridge, MA: Cowley Publications, 2001).

2. Dietrich Bonhoeffer, *The Cost of Discipleship*, rev. ed. (New York: Collier Books, 1959), 45–47, 99.

Week Four

1. The term *Parousia* refers to Jesus' second coming; we say in the Apostles' Creed, "[He] will come again to judge the living and the dead" (Ecumenical Version).

2. From a lecture given at Myers Park United Methodist Church, Charlotte, North Carolina, on March 9, 2009. This and other insights are available in Dr. Gilbert R. Rendle's books, among them *Leading Change in the Congregation: Spiritual and Organizational Tools for Leaders* (Bethesda, MD: Alban Institute, 1998).

About the Author

THOMAS R. (Tom) STEAGALD (STEE-gald) embraces the appellation "garden-variety preacher." With and among glad, generous, and hard-working saints, he tends a green acre of God's kingdom in Shelby, North Carolina: Lafayette Street United Methodist Church. Tom has also served churches in Tennessee and Kentucky. He often preaches at revivals and camp meetings and for ten years has been adjunct professor at the Hood Theological Seminary in Salisbury, North Carolina.

A widely published writer, Tom's articles, reviews, sermons, and commentary have appeared in *The Christian Century, The United Methodist Reporter, ethicsdaily, Preaching, The Journal of Biblical Preaching, The Upper Room Disciplines, Homiletics, Feasting on the Word, The Abingdon Preaching Annual.* He has authored three previous books.

Tom's theological education took him to the Southern Baptist Theological Seminary (MDiv) and the Candler School of Theology, Emory University (DMin). He has done additional study at Wake Forest University.

Tom is married to Jo, who serves as minister to children and families at the River Hills Community Church in Lake Wylie, South Carolina. They have two children—Bethany, a therapist for children with autism, and Jacob, a soon-to-be graduate student in New Testament. A bulldog puppy, Dudley, and a neurotic dachshund, Dunkin, work hard to keep all members of the family agile.